Analytics in Healthcare:
An Introduction

Edited by
Raymond A. Gensinger, Jr., MD, CPHIMS, FHIMSS

Contributors
James Adams, MBA
James E. Gaston, MBA, FHIMSS
David Garets, FHIMSS
Genevieve B. Melton, MD, FACS, FASCRS
Kim Ott
György J. Simon, PhD
Detlev H. Smaltz, PhD, FHIMSS, FACHE
Samuel VanNorman, MBA, CPHQ
Nathaniel A. Wells, MHI

HIMSS Mission
To globally lead endeavors optimizing health engagements and care outcomes through information technology.

Requests for permission to reproduce any part of this work should be sent to:
Permissions Editor
HIMSS
33 W. Monroe St., Ste. 1700
Chicago, IL 60603
nancy.vitucci@himssmedia.com

ISBN: 978-1-938904-64-6

For more information about HIMSS, please visit www.himss.org.

About the Editor

Raymond A. Gensinger, Jr., MD, CPHIMS, FHIMSS and diplomate of Clinical Informatics is the Chief Medical Information Officer (CMIO) for Fairview Health Services, an integrated delivery network in Minnesota. As CMIO, Dr. Gensinger is responsible for Fairview's clinical information technology transformation strategy. He has held similar roles at the Hennepin County Medical Center in Minneapolis. He is also a general internist and holds appointments as an assistant professor of internal medicine, affiliate faculty of the School of Nursing, and faculty of the Institute for Health Informatics at the University of Minnesota. At Fairview, Dr. Gensinger chairs the Institutional Informatics Steering Committee, as well as provides oversight for all other clinical information acquisitions and decisions. He is a past chair of the Minnesota Epic Users Group, director for HIE-Bridge, the Minnesota health information exchange and serves on the Minnesota e-Health Initiative Advisory Committee. He is a past president of the Minnesota chapter of HIMSS and served as a director of HIMSS from 2004 to 2007. Dr. Gensinger has written or presented on more than 50 healthcare information systems–related topics. He is the editor of *Introduction to Healthcare Information Enabling Technologies* and received a Healthcare Informatics Innovator Award from *Modern Healthcare* magazine in September 2006.

About the Contributors

James Adams, MBA leads the Health Care IT Suite for The Advisory Board Company. His areas of expertise include business strategic planning and implementation; executive and board communication strategies; IT-enabled accountable care and population health management; IT strategic planning and implementation; IT value assessments; and business intelligence and analytics strategies. Prior to joining The Advisory Board Company, he was executive director of IBM's Center for Health Care Management, which focused on global thought leadership for health care. Prior to joining IBM through an acquisition, Mr. Adams was a senior leader at Healthlink and Gartner and he has C-suite experience in a multiple industries. He is a frequent speaker on strategic healthcare and healthcare IT topics. He holds a bachelor's degree summa cum laude in mathematics from Texas Tech University and an MBA from the University of Phoenix, where he received the outstanding student award.

James E. Gaston, MBA, FHIMSS has more than 23 years of healthcare information technology experience with both provider and payor organizations. Currently Mr. Gaston serves as the Senior Director of Clinical and Business Intelligence for HIMSS Analytics, a cause-based, not-for-profit organization exclusively focused on providing global leadership for the optimal use of information technology (IT) and management systems for the betterment of healthcare. In this role Mr. Gaston facilitates primary market research, white paper research and publication, and speaks as an expert on the use of both clinical and business intelligence (C&BI) and analytics in healthcare. Mr. Gaston is responsible for the new international DELTA Powered™ Analytics Assessment, maturity model roadmap, and associated certification program, which will compliment and extend the value proposition HIMSS Analytics offers to healthcare providers (www.HIMSSAnalytics.org/DELTA). Mr. Gaston has an MBA and a bachelor's of science degree in computer science engineering from the University of Arkansas. He previously served as president of the Arkansas chapter of HIMSS.

David Garets, FHIMSS is a principal at Mountain Summit Advisors, providing mergers and acquisitions, recapitalization/financing, and consulting services to private healthcare IT firms. He's also an advisor and chair of the executive advisory board for SCI Solutions, as well as a senior advisor for Next Wave Connect. Previously, he served as president and CEO of HIMSS Analytics, Executive Vice President of HIMSS, and has held executive positions at Healthlink and Gartner. Mr. Garets served as HIMSS board chair in 2004. He sits on the governing boards of Health Care DataWorks and the PeaceHealth Northwest Network. He was a charter member of CHIME and served on the faculties of the CHIME Information Management Executive courses for 11 years. He is an internationally known author and speaker on healthcare information strategies and technologies, and in 2011 was elected to the HIMSS 50-in-50, the 50 most memorable and influential contributors to healthcare IT in the last 50 years. Mr. Garets is the co-creator of the HIMSS Analytics EMR Adoption Model, the international de facto standard for measuring the progress toward a full electronic medical record. Mr. Garets earned a bachelor's degree in business administration in marketing from Texas Tech University.

Genevieve B. Melton, MD, FACS, FASCRS is an associate professor of surgery and core faculty in the Institute for Health Informatics at University of Minnesota and Chief Medical Information Officer for University of Minnesota Physicians. After bachelor's preparation in mathematics, electrical engineering and computer science at Washington University, she completed medical school and surgical training at Johns Hopkins, a colorectal surgery fellowship at Cleveland Clinic, and a postdoctoral National Library of Medicine biomedical informatics fellowship at Columbia University. Currently, her informatics research focuses on the development and application of biomedical standards and clinical natural language processing techniques to clinical problems. Dr. Melton has written more than 75 peer-reviewed publications and is Principal Investigator on informatics research grants through the National Library of Medicine and Agency for Healthcare Research and Quality. Dr. Melton co-directs the Clinical Natural Language Processing Program of Excellence and serves on the Informatics Key Function Committee for the Clinical Translational Science Award at University of Minnesota. She also serves on the Clinical Informatics Subspecialty Committee of the American Board of Preventative Medicine, the American College of Surgeons Informatics Committee, and the American Medical Informatics Association Working Group Steering Committee.

Kim Ott leverages a 30+ year career in Healthcare Information Technology where she has engaged in a variety of disciplines, including application design and development, database administration, operating systems maintenance, data integration, data warehouse development, and business intelligence and analytics delivery. Prior to this experience, she spent three years studying as a nurse at the University of Minnesota before going on to earn an associate's degree in data processing at Western Wisconsin Technical College and a bachelor's degree in information technology at American Intercontinental University. As a Director of Information Technology at Fairview Health Services, she combines a clinical healthcare knowledge with technical expertise to lead a team of 100 IT professionals. Since 2005, her passion has been driving business intelligence and data warehousing strategies at Fairview Health Services. Kim lives in Cambridge, Minnesota on a small hobby farm with her husband and her four horses.

György J. Simon, PhD, is a clinical assistant professor at the Institute for Health Informatics, University of Minnesota. Dr. Simon is a data mining and statistics expert with a research interest in developing and applying data mining methodologies toward discovering novel ways to improve healthcare. Before joining the University of Minnesota, Dr. Simon was a researcher at Mayo Clinic, focusing on clinical data mining and analysis of genomic and image data. Previously, he worked for Yahoo Inc. in the area of big data analytics and modeling applied to web search.

Detlev H. (Herb) Smaltz, PhD, FHIMSS, FACHE is the founder and former chair and CEO of Health Care DataWorks, Inc., an Ohio State University technology commercialization company. He works with healthcare provider organizations to more strategically leverage data analytics and business intelligence to improve their organizational performance. Health Care DataWorks is a provider of enterprise data warehouse and business intelligence tools and strategic enterprise consulting services. Prior to founding Health Care DataWorks, he served as the CIO of the Ohio State University Medical Center. In that role, he led an IT organization. In addition, he served as an associate vice president for health sciences, leading collaborative initiatives among the three mission areas of the medical center: research, academics and patient care. Dr. Smaltz has more than 25 years' experience in healthcare management. He is a Fellow of the Healthcare Information and Management Systems Society (FHIMSS) and served on the HIMSS Board of Directors from 2002 to 2005 and as the HIMSS 2004–2005 Vice Chair. In addition he is a Fellow in the American College of Healthcare Executives (FACHE). His recent publications include *Information Systems for Healthcare Management, 8th Edition*, with Gerald Glandon and Donna Slovensky; *The Healthcare Information Technology Planning Fieldbook*, with George "Buddy" Hickman; and *The Executive's Guide to Electronic Health Records* with E. Berner.

Samuel VanNorman, MBA, CPHQ is the senior health economics director for Optum Health's Collaborative Care group, working with provider organizations around the country on economics and analytics programs focused on improving value in healthcare. VanNorman has a wide-ranging background in healthcare, including work in finance, operations, quality improvement, innovation, and economics at payer, provider, and consulting organizations. He has also served on a variety of state and national advisory committees on topics including ACOs, population health management, analytics and quality. VanNorman also teaches graduate health economics at Saint Cloud State University. Prior to working in healthcare, he designed microchips for IBM and several failed start-ups. He holds a bachelor's degree in computer engineering from Purdue University, a master's degree in business administration from the University of North Carolina, and a master's of science in health services research from the University of Minnesota (completion in early 2014).

Nathaniel A. Wells, MHI earned a bachelor's degree in computer forensics at Metropolitan State University. He went on to earn his master's degree in health informatics from the University of Minnesota's Institute for Health Informatics as a University Partnership for Health Informatics scholar. Wells started his career in the healthcare industry at Fairview Health Services in the provider employment department of human resources, later making the switch to the revenue cycle area. He aims to use innovative approaches, diverse experiences, data interpretation, problem solving, technology, and education to help improve patient care through supporting healthcare providers. When not working, he can be found volunteering, fishing, solving puzzles, fixing computers, and spending time with his family. You can contact him on LinkedIn at www.linkedin.com/in/mrwells60.

Contents

Foreword

Thomas H. Davenport

President's Distinguished Professor of IT and Management, Babson College
Fellow, MIT Center for Digital Business
Co-Founder and Director of Research, International Institute for Analytics
Senior Advisor, Deloitte Analytics

This book, a compendium addressing various important aspects of healthcare analytics, is both symbolic of a dramatic change in healthcare and a major step forward in itself. The dramatic change in the industry is nothing less than a revolution based on the use of analytics and data for healthcare decision making.

The revolution is sorely needed. Healthcare in the United States and, to some degree elsewhere in the world, has a major problem: we pay too much for the care we receive. Our healthcare bill is approaching 20% of the gross domestic product in the United States, and we are in the middle of the pack at best in terms of care outcomes such as life expectancy, infant mortality, and likelihood of acquiring chronic diseases.

Simply put, the primary reason for this situation is that we make bad decisions for patients. We give them care that they don't need or that does not benefit them. We fail to connect the costs of treatments with their benefits. We don't combine all the information we have about patients to diagnose their conditions, monitor their progress, and recommend ongoing care patterns. New science and care protocols emerge daily, leading to more complexity than most practitioners can comprehend. Every dramatic new development, from personalized genetic medicine to robotics and telemedicine, opens up new frontiers and provides more data, but this can further confuse patients and their caregivers.

People make poor decisions in other industries, but such decisions generally result only in wasted money, failed strategies, and frustrated customers. In healthcare, poor decision making may lead to loss of a patient's life, the imposition of pain and suffering, or even financial desperation. Nowhere in modern life is there more incentive to improve decision processes and outcomes than in healthcare.

There is some good news amidst all these negatives, and it's chronicled in this book. One of the most powerful new developments in healthcare is the use of analytics to help make clinical, operational, and financial decisions. This new toolset has the potential to shed considerable light on the entire terrain of the industry. When executed well, analytics can document which treatments work for which patients, who is likely to acquire particular diseases, and how much a treatment protocol should—and does—cost. Data and statistics can shed light on which provider organizations, and even which individual providers, are doing a good job. They can even begin to bridge the large gaps between industry subsegments (e.g., hospitals, physician practices, home health). In many cases today, no single individual or institution is even accountable for all decisions made on a patient's behalf. Integrated data and analytics are beginning to provide a much more comprehensive perspective on patient care processes, spending, and outcomes. In short, healthcare is poised on the edge of an analytics-driven transformation.

HIMSS and HIMSS Analytics have been instrumental in the widespread adoption of electronic health records, and that data source is increasingly forming a solid base for analytics. Knowing what patients spent what time in the hospital or doctor's office, what treatments they received, and how well they recovered are all critical to effective clinical decision making. When the records also include financial and billing information, providers can begin to understand the value equation: whether patients or their insurers are receiving adequate value for their spending.

This promise is rapidly becoming a reality for many hospitals. Organizations that have reached Stage 7—the highest level in the HIMSS Analytics Electronic Medical Record (EMR) Adoption Model—not only have fully installed their EMR systems and used them to replace paper charts, but they are using the data for better decisions. In HIMSS Analytics' terms, they "use data warehousing and mining techniques to capture and analyze care data to perfect, advance and institute organization-wide operational, financial and quality improvements." This is great progress toward healthcare analytics success. Of note, 160 hospitals in the United States alone have achieved Stage 7 as of the end of 2013.

The problem, of course, is that neither the business environment nor the information environment of healthcare institutions remains static. Those hospitals that have mastered EMR data are now moving on to try to incorporate insurance claims data, self-reported data from patients, data from consumer activity and health tracking devices, and even genomic data into their analytical models and initiatives. Those hospitals that prospered in a fee-for-service environment are now attempting to adapt their processes and analytics to an accountable care or capitated model. Further, the pace of mergers and acquisitions among healthcare providers continues apace. All of this change means that today's analytical leaders in healthcare must never rest in their journeys and must continue innovating in many respects. As Chapter 3 in the book points out, even the best providers are only at base camp in a long mountain climb.

Despite these challenges, this book presents clear evidence that the state of the art in the field is gaining sophistication, approaching the analytical capabilities of other leading industries. Just to give a few examples, Chapter 5 reports on attempts to mine EMR data for patterns and trends. Chapter 6 reports on organizational structures that providers are establishing to support business intelligence and analytics. Chapter 7 describes an important underlying capability for analytics: data governance. Finally, Chapter 8 describes a new initiative to benchmark analytical capabilities that is a joint venture of HIMSS Analytics and the International Institute for Analytics, an organization I co-founded in 2010. These are only a few of the exciting developments that this book contains.

The field of healthcare analytics may be only at base camp, but the climb has started and the climbers are rapidly gaining altitude. We may have labored in the foothills for far too long, but there is little doubt that we will eventually reach great heights. We cannot yet see the summit, but we know which way is up. Healthcare undeniably will be transformed for the better by analytics, and if you want to know how the transformation will happen and how to ensure your place in it, keep reading.

Preface

Raymond A. Gensinger, Jr., MD, CPHIMS, FHIMSS

Analytics in Healthcare: An Introduction is intended to help you get off the bench and onto the analytics playing field. Each of the authors brings varied experiences and perspectives to his or her writing. Each has some level of responsibility for analytics in his or her organization. Some are responsible for executing and harvesting value from the advanced systems we have implemented and the data that those systems collect or generate. Others, who assist in the development of analytics or teach about analytics in a consultancy role, have considerable past experiences directly building advanced analytics programs. Regardless of our current responsibilities, we realized that we wanted to help you make a difference in healthcare.

The murky domain of analytics (or heaven forbid the specter of "big data") is cluttered with exceedingly high expectations and is just foreign enough to most of us to be a frightening arena to enter. The authors hope to scale back the hype and provide a level of clarity in both your understanding and approach to analytics in healthcare. If you are a student, we hope that you will understand the opportunity that is available to you as a potential career choice along several career paths. If you are a staff member within a healthcare organization, we hope this book can provide a good starting point, whether as a source to clarify your opportunities, a manageable place to start, a bit of a roadmap, or the reference to getting started with HIMSS Analytics.

We have purposely kept the book both short and at a high level to make this a quick and manageable read. Our desire is for you to move through the book quickly and begin to build your analytics program. Each of the authors has much more to say than the words here, and we welcome any opportunities to correspond and help direct you further.

We would like to acknowledge the contributions of others who have helped make this work possible:

- Kristine Vnuck was instrumental in keeping us organized and together as we virtually constructed our materials.
- The Advisory Board Company shared its personnel and intellectual content.
- Mayo Clinic researchers Pedro J. Caraballo, MD, M. Regina Castro, MD, Peter W. Li, PhD, and Jyotishman Pathak, PhD, contributed to data mining knowledge.

Thank you, learn, and enjoy.

Raymond A. Gensinger, Jr., MD CPHIMS, FHIMSS
Diplomate of Clinical Informatics

Chapter 1

A Healthcare Analytics Roadmap

Raymond A. Gensinger, Jr.

If you've picked up this book in search of pearls, you are seeking to understand how to build a program of analytics to better your organization. We are all trying to answer some of the following questions:

- Do I really understand the business of healthcare to the fullest extent necessary?
- Am I prepared to answer the really hard questions about the safety, quality, cost, and experience of care that is being delivered?
- Why do the retail, revolving credit, hospitality, and Internet industries know more about assessing patterns and predicting the necessary next actions than does the healthcare industry today?

These represent only the beginning of what seems to be a seemingly infinite number of complicated questions that must be addressed by the healthcare industry RIGHT NOW. The reasons that the time is now for healthcare are detailed at length by the authors in this book, but we'll introduce them in this chapter.

THE QUALITY AND COST PARADIGM

In the fall of 2012, *Consumer Reports* examined quality and cost of healthcare based on data from primary care clinics in the Minnesota Community Measurement Program that were collected by HealthPartners.[1] The methodology for the program can be found at Minnesota HealthScores.[2] According to the article, there were not always strong correlations between the quality of care provided and its cost. When these data were combined, patients could assess the value of the care they could expect to receive at these clinics. Of note, different clinics within the same care system could have relatively wide variations in quality of care provided.

This report reflects the changing healthcare paradigm and highlights that all healthcare organizations (HCOs) must either "up their game" to understand the services they are providing or at least begin to learn how to "get into the game" in the first place. HCOs that do not pursue one of these options will have great difficulty in surviving.

Many HCOs are highly effective at descriptive analytics that involve gathering data from their organization and creating representations of the results in tabular or graphic formats. The problem has been that the data were often manually extracted from charts. Transcribers would re-create clinical data entered by nurses, physicians, or other care providers in handwritten notes. Health information management (HIM) staff and coders would translate this information for billing purposes or eventually to help support the justification of admissions through utilization management personnel. Regardless of the end purpose, the process typically included: manual documentation > manual transcription > manual entry into a database or spreadsheet > graphic representation of the results to support the business. Once represented, operational managers and leaders would combine the findings with their experiences in an attempt to project future decisions on construction, staffing, treatment plans, and personnel evaluations.

Such descriptions now seem archaic, given all that we know and can do today. They served our organizations adequately despite the intensity of personnel use required for these manual processes. However, advances in clinical care, clinical computing, and payer sophistication as well as the diverse specialization of providers has made advanced computing and analytics a necessity in today's healthcare paradigm.

ANALYTICS FOR QUALITY

"Quality" and "safety" are the battle cries for moving the analytics mission forward. Consider the safety perspective of drug recalls, one of the most common yet challenging problems faced by HCOs over the past 30 years. No more than 20 years ago, a drug recall required that a clinician or system review every individual chart to find those patients receiving the particular medication and identify whether a patient had experienced the potential medication/medication or medication/problem interaction. In some cases, the only effective method for identifying these patients was to work backward from the pharmacy, gathering information on patients who had been prescribed a medication and then notifying prescribing physicians of their affected patients. Those lists then would need to be cross-referenced with patient charts to validate that individual patients were still receiving the medication, and the clinician would need to reach out to each patient.

Today's analytic tools provide a much faster and more thorough understanding of patients and perhaps even correct identification of comorbid conditions or situations that make one population of patients more prone to an adverse reaction or outcome than another population. Answering these questions becomes paramount in a healthcare environment advancing at a pace that is no longer comprehensible by individuals, as suggested by the growing healthcare literature (Figure 1-1). At the point in time covered in this graph, the growth rate was still linear. Druss and Marcus[3] suggested at the time that clinicians develop active reading skills, watch for prefiltered materials such as reviews and guidelines, and focus on peer-reviewed materials. Today, with the addition of genotypic data to accompany phenotypic data, we may be approaching a logarithmic knowledge growth rate.

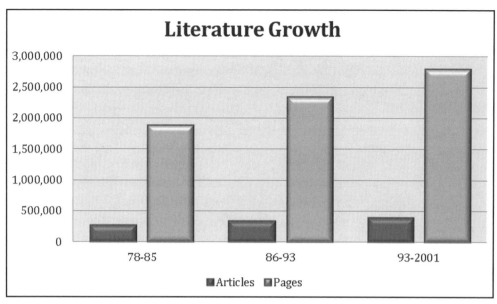

Figure 1-1: Growth in number of scientific articles and total pages. Data from Druss and Marcus.[3]

ASSESSMENTS OF VARIATION

An ongoing challenge between providers and the organizations that employ or host them with medical staff membership is that not all clinicians enter the practice of medicine with the intent of high-quality patient care. Some clinicians expect practice autonomy with very little restriction. Hospitals where they have privileges or the payers with whom they contract might request evidence of their experience in completing certain procedures or care experiences. However, in the past that documentation had no requisite expectation of the quality or outcome of those events. Additionally, once granted those privileges, organizations typically have not required ongoing documentation of the providers' continued skill or expertise in those privileges.

A typical medical resident applying for new privileges at a hospital likely would have little difficulty documenting the number of times he or she performed central line placements or sigmoidoscopies, managed cardiac arrest, and treated patients with fulminant hepatic or renal failure. However, opportunities to maintain these skills may be limited in practice when the need for such skills becomes infrequent or rare. At what point are skills lost? At what point does the practitioner lose touch with the appropriate standard of care for a particular acute illness?

Internal medicine and family medicine subspecialties offer board certification, with recertification required at 10 and 7 years, respectively. The recertification process can demonstrate a clinician's ongoing cognitive skills, but physical skills generally are not tested. Insurance carriers have regularly required their providers to maintain a level of expertise demonstrated by an active board certification, but they do not necessarily offer a method of tracking procedural skills.

In 2006, The Joint Commission introduced the ongoing professional practice evaluation (OPPE). This evaluation required organizations to perform continuous monitor-

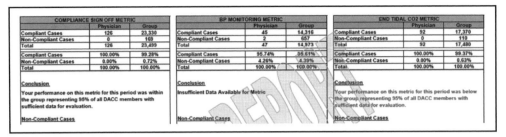

Figure 1-2: Sample OPPE Report. (Reprinted with permission from Ehrenfeld, et al.[4])

ing of their medical staff's performance, quality, and safety as a standard requirement for maintaining privileges (Figure 1-2).

Depending on the technologic infrastructure of an organization, collection and representation of such measures was a labor-intensive chore that was misunderstood (because many Joint Commission standards and expectations are not clearly understood by the typical medical staff member), challenged (because the summarized results were the work of members of a quality or HIM department), or deemed time irrelevant (because the data might represent cases as much as 6 to 12 months old, depending on the sources of the data and elapsed time for organization and representation).

With more sophisticated electronic health record (EHR) infrastructure than was available in 2006, the healthcare industry is much better prepared to deliver not only more timely data but much more comprehensive data that can quickly "link" to the EHR and patient actions. According to the United States Department of Health and Human Services, more than 80% of hospitals have achieved the standards to qualify for health information technology incentives (Figure 1-3).[5]

The use of analytic tools can supply the quality assurance (QA) department and providers with a far better understanding of patients within their report profile, compare providers with their peers, and compare patients with patients of peers. In addition, providers may gain a more detailed understanding of not just the point in time represented by the scorecard but also meaningful follow-up information regarding outcomes, patient satisfaction, and total costs of care for the patient within the reporting window and beyond.

WHAT IS BIG DATA?

In an article published in the *New York Times*, Steve Lohr[6] traced the expression "big data" to Silicon Graphics' chief scientist John R. Mashey as part of a presentation given in April 1998.[7] Mashey was examining several technologies that were being affected by the impending growth in volumes of data accumulated and distributed within organizations and across the Internet. His focus was on the impact of such large volumes of data.

Many in the healthcare technology business use the term "big data" to conjure fear and create a call to action. Big data is portrayed as a problem to be solved, an animal to be tamed, or perhaps even an innovation that must be adopted. For anyone who has ever visited the medical records room of a large academic medical center, the concept of big data conjures up a visual image in search of a caption (Figure 1-4). A single chart

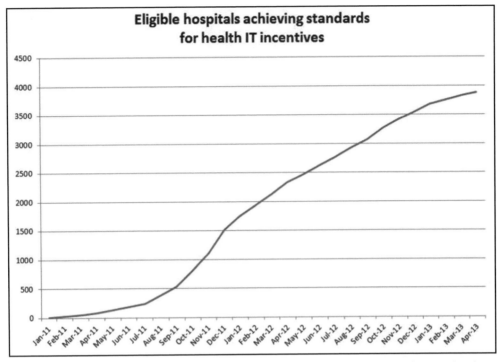

Figure 1-3: Eligible hospitals achieving standards for health information technology incentives. From U.S. Department of Health and Human Services.[5]

could contain thousands of pages representing dozens of clinical domains of data supplied by care providers across a wide geography that is accessible only to savvy HIM staffers or the clinical care personnel. Thus, in reality, healthcare has been suffering from a "big data" problem for decades.

If the problem has been present for decades, why is big data an issue that is particularly pertinent for healthcare systems today? The answer is that providers are finally in a position to actually do something about the volumes and variety of data through systems and tools that can harvest and analyze the data. What is now needed is a solution to the accelerating velocity at which that data are being created. A further call to action is that other adjacent healthcare industries, such as pharmaceuticals, insurance, and biotechnology, are well ahead of care providers in effectively gathering, analyzing, and repurposing the limited subsets of data that are available to them. For the most part, the entire healthcare system now is required to process data as fast as or faster than these adjacent industries. Beyond processing the data, providers need to understand and act on it at levels of performance that are foreign to them. There is little reason why any individual HCO should not be able to calculate its own findings on the lowest-cost and highest-value medications in the management of particular disease, care plans that are most effective for a patient's disease profile, or the most appropriate biomedical device to implant in an individual patient's hip.

The adaptive changes through which an HCO must go before being prepared to handle any analytics are many and complicated. This can be referred to as the challenges over "little data," which is well summarized by Dan Munro in *Forbes*.[8] Munro

Figure 1-4: Medical records in a clinician's office.

points out, for example, numerous problems with how data are represented at the most local of levels, a unit of patient care, which illustrate the difficult path that the healthcare industry faces. Clearly, the industry must resolve many other issues before addressing the hype of big data.

HEALTH MAINTENANCE AND ACCOUNTABILITY

Healthcare reform and healthcare finance reform continue to place pressure on the industry. The popular health maintenance organizations (HMOs) and managed care organizations of the 1990s have been transformed into the accountable care organizations (ACOs) of the current era. Although HMOs and ACOs have similar ultimate goals, the size of the programs differs considerably. HMOs are typically based on very large populations of patients that allow the risk to be diluted; ACOs may be large or support populations as small as 5,000 participants. Many of Medicare's pioneer ACO programs average 25,000 lives. As the numbers decrease, understanding and managing the risk for those populations must become substantially more precise to ensure program solvency. A single case of unexpectedly expensive care in a small population can mean the difference between profitability and a program deficit.

During their heyday, the HMO model was focused on managing costs. This was achieved by managing access through the primary care provider's roles and responsibilities. At the time, the quality and value of the services were presumed to be high and the point of demarcation was inappropriate utilization of specialty services either

Table 1-1: Payment Model Comparison

	Fee-for-service	Health Maintenance Organization	Accountable Care Organization
At-risk Party	Patient	Payer	Provider
Patient Choice	Unlimited	Primary care gatekeepers	Unlimited
Quality Expectations	Patient	Set by payers	Set by providers
Experience Expectations	Set by patient	Set by payer	Set by provider
Provider Focus	Patient care	Cost containment	Value and quality
Benchmark	None	Cost control	Quality benchmarks
Controls	None	Must stay in network	None

procedurally or cognitively through referrals. Payers had good visibility of the total cost of care through their claims management processes, yet providers could only see their own claims information. Their only options were to control access. Program collapse was no surprise. Patient experience and quality were compromised at the expense of resource management.

With the replacement of HMOs by ACOs, primary care providers are being augmented with care managers. What is the difference (Table 1-1)? Fundamentally, healthcare systems and providers are actually equipped to address patient experience and quality/value as they were not in the past. Organizations have the data and analytic potential to answer very complicated questions about the total cost of care that can guide them in better managing their patient populations. Additionally, they have an improved ability to segment patients into risk categories by several measures, including disease classification and disease burden. The data exist for an organization to answer questions about the total cost of care, not just within their own organization but across any of the organizations where a patient receives care. In part, this results from a closer partnership between provider organizations and payers (Centers for Medicare & Medicaid Services and others) that supports the full claims transparency necessary for an accountable provider or organization to understand the total cost of care.

Today's ACOs have the power to go beyond claims data that are latent and often incomplete. ACOs can harness real-time data from the EHR and other local data sources to categorize patients in their populations as well as understand more about the patient outcomes achieved. Thus, ACOs can determine if a higher cost of inpatient care actually pays future dividends for an outpatient who has higher levels of mobility, fewer complications, or generalized higher satisfaction than could be measured before.

Further, all of the providers are working directly with an automated system of care in their daily work. The knowledge that is derived from the analytics can potentially be returned to those individuals in real time. Prompts, alerts, and all means of decision support or practice direction can be delivered at a point in time when the action can make a difference in patient outcomes through enhanced process measurements.

BENCHMARKING

Earlier QA reporting results were suggestive of historical points in time and typically were derived from financially driven billing codes. As organizational data mature, more data are reported to operational and clinical leaders. In contrast to the previously noted financial reports, data are now more recent (although sometimes still months old) and perhaps are presented in a model as sophisticated as a run chart (Figure 1-5). Such a chart effectively describes the organizational measures of interest, but the answer to the inevitable question of whether local performance compares to a community norm or standard remains absent. If data cannot be compared to that of local peers, many will question what those peers are experiencing.

An opportunity exists for improving any measure internally, but the value of making a comparison with a similar group allows for better decisions about where to begin changes or where to make the greatest investments to improve further. A well-defined peer group can also assist in determining where to look for help in an attempt to jump-start an initiative.

In a large academic medical center full of trainees and many complex research initiatives, understanding how best to optimize a process of admitting a patient and wading through the medication reconciliation process can be difficult. A good understanding of the efficiency of the process and the measure of patient experience is very important in comparison to the local community hospital, but equally important is comparison to a similar academic medical center in the neighboring state or region.

One approach to accessing to a wider comparative group is participation in registries. Registries were initiated to track deaths and disease but have evolved greatly. In 1992, Congress established the Cancer Registries Amendment Act in an effort to collect cancer data from all states to gain greater understanding of the disease and develop bet-

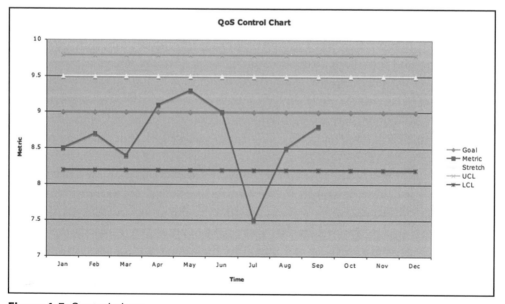

Figure 1-5: Control chart.

ter policies. Following a common set of data standards, vocabulary, and data definitions created a valuable database. This is now a core tool in cancer research.

Registries exist for many other disease categories. Many subspecialty medical organizations have created and defined registries to support research and QA and used them to determine centers of excellence for disease care and management. These registries help the public understand which providers and organizations meet professionally agreed-upon minimum standards of care and outcomes for a variety of healthcare events, such as myocardial infarction and stroke, or highly complicated and integrated medical conditions such as bariatric care.

In an age of analytics, benchmarking is just the starting point for organizational opportunity. As an example, consider the application of analytics to the problem of readmissions and their negative economic impact. The control chart in Figure 1-5 could be a run chart of readmission rates. A readmission is an outcome that has many preceding factors and events that make it understandable and perhaps both predictable and preventable. The analytics and data mining techniques described in this book can be used to find clusters of events that predict readmission. These events can be monitored using patient-focused "sensors" that trigger alerts for a care coordinator, summarized on a daily report of high-risk patients, or even used to create a queue of prescribed interventions that should be taken in an effort to reverse the potential readmission pathway for an individual patient.

CHANGES IN HEALTHCARE ACUITY

Managing the complexity of any individual patient in the hospital has always been complicated, requiring the interactions and services of physicians, nurses, pharmacists, therapists, and social workers among others. However, changing acuity of the hospital population has had a serious impact on operations. A young adult with acute appendicitis, a pregnant woman at term, and even an elderly person with pneumonia represent straightforward presentations that should be easily managed when the patients are admitted to the hospital. On the other end of the spectrum are patients who experience fevers of unknown origin, elderly patients who have septicemia, and elderly patients who have diabetes and acute myocardial infarctions. Historically, they were rapidly admitted to the hospital and often had the luxury of nearly unlimited lengths of stay while clinicians determined their problems, defined treatment approaches, and educated patients and family before discharge.

Today's economic pressures that encourage fewer admissions, direct more observation stays, and deny payment for readmissions within 30 days combine to increase the complexity of case management. In this environment, rapid decision making is the expectation rather than the exception. The general patient population is older (Figure 1-6),[9] has more complicated multifaceted disease profiles (diabetes + hypertension + obesity + heart disease + renal disease + dementia), and is managed across a larger number of specialty providers, each of whom is focused on only a single disease category. Further, medicine continues to learn that sociodemographic elements contribute to the understanding, diagnosis, and treatment of disease.[10]

Age, urgency, complexity, and cost pressure all contribute to the acuity of current medical care. Leveraging the power of analytic tools may facilitate the management of

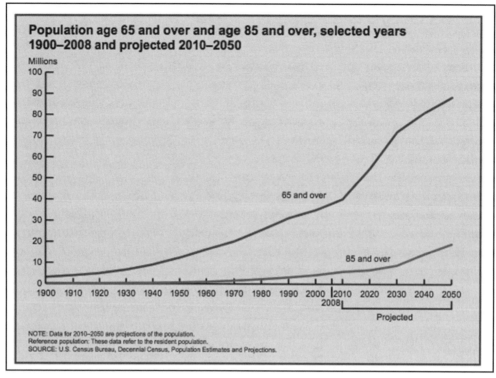

Figure 1-6: The aging United States population.

such patients by optimizing their care within necessary economic boundaries. Although every patient is unique, large databases offer a better opportunity to find "patients like mine" to understand or learn about potential diagnostic pathways (e.g., influenza has arrived in the community), treatment programs (e.g., patients of differing ethnic origins respond differently to common medications), or even limiting sociodemographic factors of the patient (e.g., patient may not have access to much healthy food or have limited access to the nearest rehabilitation programs via public transit services).

A key aspect of care for high-acuity patients is to identify elements that are both variable (where deterioration is likely to worsen the condition) and controllable (body weight, blood glucose). Once identified, clinicians can enter those elements in a patient monitoring tool/process to ensure appropriate follow-up and tracking of the patient. Effective monitoring and the tools associated with the collection and calculation of effects of change can trigger alerts for intervention from a care coordinator (predictive analytics) or suggest an intervention (prescriptive analytics) directly to the patient (come in for a clinic visit today) in an effort to prevent a follow-up emergency department visit or hospital readmission.

VIRTUAL CARE OPPORTUNITIES

Virtual care and remote patient monitoring have been in existence for decades. The remote monitoring of astronauts in the space program during the 1960s was the first concentrated virtual healthcare program. Monitoring of heart rhythm and pacemaker

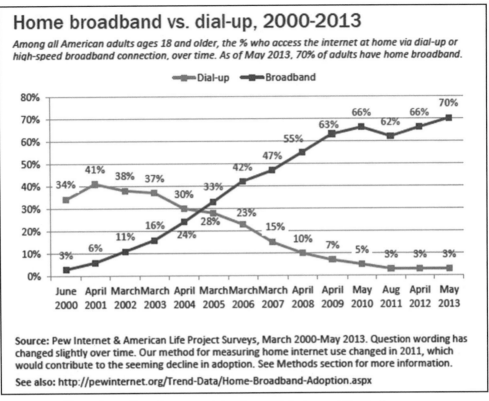

Figure 1-7: Home broadband connectivity. From Zickuhr and Smith.[11]

functions was the predominant remote monitoring technique that followed for many decades. More recently, remote monitoring capabilities have exploded.

The drivers for change are likely multifactorial. They include the acceleration of home connectivity from telephone and cable services to deep penetration of broadband Internet connectivity. As late as 2005, as many households were connecting to the Internet via standard telephone service as they were via broadband (Figure 1-7). Today, the percentages are 3% and 70%, respectively. Of the remaining 30% without broadband, many have smart phones as their only means of connecting to the Internet.

In addition to enhanced connectivity to the home, more devices in the home are capable of leveraging these connections. Smart TVs, tablet computers, laptops, desktops, smart appliances, and even smart health monitoring are becoming the norm. ABI Research estimates that the total number of wearable devices with fitness and wellness applications will grow from 16.2 million in 2011 to 93 million in 2017.[12] All of these devices make real-time connections to the Internet, cloud-based monitoring services, and potentially even directly to an individual's healthcare provider. All are opening new means of monitoring, support, and disease prevention.

Home-based smart devices and their real-time connectivity offer further sensors that can provide noninvasive monitoring of patients with chronic and debilitating disease. To date, fragile patients can add monitoring to their beds, toilets, refrigerators, scales and, with special accelerometer-adapted watches, fall detection devices. As cited by Munro,[8] "the incorporated Gartner Hype Cycle® (Stamford, CT) shows that home health monitoring is moving out of the trough of disillusionment and onto the slope of enlightenment. Sophisticated analytic algorithms will be required to monitor the volumes of incoming data, filter the signals away from the background noise, and alert and advise the care team as to when an intervention is necessary."

REFERENCES

1. Santa J. When costlier medical care isn't better, *Consumer Reports.* October 2012. http://www.consumerreports.org/cro/magazine/2012/10/when-costlier-medical-care-isn-t-better/index.htm. Accessed December 2013.

2. Quality. Value. Results. Respect. *Minnesota HealthScores.* http://mnhealthscores.org/?. Accessed September 2013.

3. Druss BG, Marcus SC. Growth and decentralization of the medical literature: implications for evidence-based medicine. *J Med Libr Assoc.* 2005;93:499-501.

4. Ehrenfeld JM, Henneman JP, Peterfreund RA, et al. Ongoing professional performance evaluation (OPPE) using automatically captured electronica anesthesia data. *Jt Comm J Qual Patient Saf.* 2012;38:73-80.

5. Doctors and hospitals' use of health IT more than doubles since 2012 [press release]. Washington, DC: United States Department of Health and Human Services; May 22, 2013. http://www.hhs.gov/news/press/2013pres/05/20130522a.html. Accessed September 2013.

6. Lohr S. The origins of 'big data': an etymological detective story. *The New York Times.* February 1, 2013. http://bits.blogs.nytimes.com/2013/02/01/the-origins-of-big-data-an-etymological-detective-story/?_r=0. Accessed December 2013.

7. Mashey JR. *Big Data...and the Next Wave of InfraStress.* http://static.usenix.org/event/usenix99/invited_talks/mashey.pdf. Accessed September 2013.

8. Munro D. Healthcare's big problem with little data. *Forbes.* April 28, 2013. http://www.forbes.com/sites/danmunro/2013/04/28/big-problem-with-little-data/. Accessed October 2013.

9. Villavicencio F. Identity in healthcare: a diet for 2011 and beyond. *The Identropy Blog.* 2011. http://blog.identropy.com/IAM-blog/bid/63526/Identity-in-Healthcare-A-Diet-for-2011-and-Beyond-Part-1-of-3. Accessed October 2013.

10. van Ryn M, Burke J. The effect of patient race and socio-economic status on physicians' perceptions of patients. *Soc Sci Med.* 2000;50:813-828.

11. Zickuhr K, Smith A. Home broadband 2013: trends and demographic differences in home broadband adoption. *Pew Internet & American Life Project.* 2013. http://www.pewinternet.org/Reports/2013/Broadband/Findings.aspx. Accessed October 2013.

12. Wang J. How Fitbit is cashing in on the high-tech fitness trend. *Entrepreneur.* July 27, 2012. http://www.entrepreneur.com/article/223780#ixzz2gd9oRUFw. Accessed October 2013.

CHAPTER 2

The Healthcare Analytics Evolution: Moving from Descriptive to Predictive to Prescriptive

James Adams and David Garets

If there were ever a need to "shine a light on the path" of a technology, the healthcare analytics and business intelligence (BI) environment has that need. Nothing in healthcare is easy or uncomplicated, but the applications, technology, and culture change surrounding analytics and BI take such complexity to a new level. How did we get to where we are and where do we need to go and why?

HISTORICAL PERSPECTIVE

Most healthcare organizations (HCOs) have made significant investments in transactional information systems that help "operate the business," including clinical systems (e.g., laboratory, radiology, pharmacy, electronic health records [EHRs]), general administrative systems (e.g., scheduling or bed management systems), revenue cycle management systems, and general financial systems (e.g., accounts payable or general ledger systems). These systems typically were initially implemented to streamline and standardize operational processes. Over time, such transactional systems have generated considerable electronic data that could be integrated and organized to ensure consistency (e.g., key data from clinical and financial systems) and then monitored and analyzed to improve performance and decision making. In the 1990s, initial attempts to integrate, monitor, and analyze data from multiple transaction systems included financial decision support systems that supported functions such as cost accounting, budgeting, and product line management as well as executive information systems that provided basic "dashboard" capabilities. These early systems seldom contained significant amounts of clinical information beyond the diagnosis-related group (DRG), International Statistical Classification of Diseases, 9th revision (ICD-9), and current procedural terminology (CPT) codes generated in conjunction with reimbursement claims.

Most industries have recognized the need for computerized decision support, but healthcare has more use cases than others. The healthcare industry is probably the most data-intensive industry on earth, generating thousands of diverse data elements hourly in most clinics and hospitals. Diseases are not simple, and comorbidities and individual health issues complicate the work of clinicians. Managing a clinical environment is complex, data intensive, and affected by significant government regulation. Business models range from all-contracted to all-employed physicians and affiliations with other providers. Added to the mix are group purchasing organizations, historic autonomous behavior on the part of physicians, a complex financing component, and customers who are loosely tethered to those who pay for healthcare services, primarily employers or the government.

Such factors suggest that healthcare would have implemented cross-industry-leading BI and analytics solutions to assist clinicians and HCO managers. Unfortunately, that has not occurred. Further, few industry terminology standards have been established, and the industry has been slow to adopt information technology (IT) to support core business processes. Finally, vendors of potentially useful systems have delivered proprietary products and have not focused, until recently, on interoperability of the data generated by them.

More than ever before, HCOs have both the need and the tools to use electronic data to improve performance and decision making. HCOs are placing much greater emphasis on performance and outcome monitoring and improving costs and quality as they develop new delivery models, such as patient-centered medical homes and accountable care organizations (ACOs) to address new reimbursement approaches and delivery requirements. Fortunately, both the data and the technology are advancing. The volume, quality, and timeliness of clinical data are exploding, with more structured clinical data anticipated in the future. Both the tools and the underlying technologies (e.g., processing power, storage capacity, network capacity, more powerful databases, and new mathematical models) have made some new types of analyses possible and other types easier or faster.

Integrating, organizing, monitoring, and analyzing data from a variety of sources can help HCOs develop more fact-based or data-based answers for many important questions such as:

- How are physicians performing in relation to costs and quality?
- What can be done to improve performance on nursing units?
- How can we improve capacity and throughput without building or modifying facilities?
- How can we identify patients during a hospital stay who are at high risk for readmission?
- How can we identify ambulatory patients who are at high risk for emergency department visits or admissions?
- Which therapeutic approaches typically work best?
- Which patients might respond best to a particular treatment?
- How can we detect problems with hospital-acquired conditions earlier?

In addition to the emergence of better tools and better technology, most HCOs also have:

- Hundreds of supported applications, most of which are not interoperable with the others, are written in proprietary languages in nonstandard architectures, and are departmentally focused
- A primary EHR system (or more than one if there has been merger and acquisition activity in the health system), implemented as a result of the American Recovery and Reinvestment Act of 2009 health information technology for economic and clinical health (HITECH) meaningful use provisions that provides consistently defined data elements across an organization and fodder for BI tools and analytics
- A heterogeneous, nonintegrated BI/analytics environment supporting reports and dashboards that are primarily departmentally focused and may have been part of another application or been purchased by less sophisticated IT buyers without a rigorous selection process
- An almost complete lack of data governance activity to define terms and the use and usability of the data, which is essential when developing an enterprise view of the HCO's data

What is the path forward?

BUSINESS INTELLIGENCE DEFINED

Various and sometimes confusing or conflicting terms are used to describe the computer-based activities used to answer the types of questions listed previously. We use "BI," an industry standard term with many different definitions, to define such activities. Somewhat more formally defined for healthcare, BI refers to the processes and technologies used to obtain timely, valuable insights into business and clinical data. The time perspective for these insights can be historical, concurrent, or prospective. The processes and technologies used by BI to analyze structured data can be segmented into three levels: descriptive, predictive, and prescriptive (Figure 2-1).

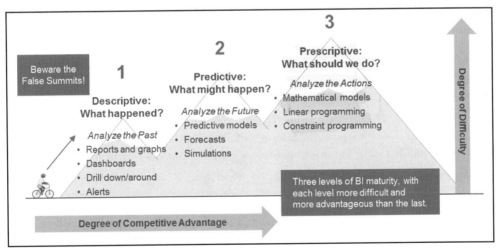

Figure 2-1: Levels of BI. From The Advisory Board Company research and analysis.

Descriptive BI

The term "BI" has historically been most closely associated with the descriptive level. At its simplest, the descriptive level includes both **standard reporting** and **ad hoc reporting**, which typically come from data and reporting capabilities contained in one transaction system. Some reporting tools independent of a specific transaction system can select, link, and report on data from multiple sources or transaction systems. More sophisticated business analysis tools and techniques bring more **advanced query** and **drilldown** capabilities.

Examining data in a number of different ways can be difficult and time consuming when using ad hoc reports. One report could be run and based on the results; additional reports could be run until obtaining the required results or determining that the required findings could not be obtained easily using an ad hoc reporting approach. Multidimensional databases can better address business analysis or query/drilldown. They are built around three key concepts: facts, dimensions, and hierarchies. A fact is an occurrence of something such as an event (e.g., a medication was prescribed or a diagnostic test was run). Dimensions define how the facts can be accessed (e.g., by patient, by doctor, or by time). Hierarchies are methods of organizing dimensions. For example, a time hierarchy could include year, quarter, and month. A physician hierarchy could include ACO, physician group practice, and individual physician.

Pivot tables, such as those in Microsoft Excel®, are very popular business analysis and data visualization tools that fit in the query and drilldown category. They are used to summarize large amounts of detailed data for intuitive understanding. A pivot table looks like any other two-dimensional table with rows and columns, but it functions very differently. The table comprises an interactive grid of nested cells, with each cell containing a single metric or calculation performed on a set of data. The contents of each cell is defined by the arrangement of the names of dimensions assigned to the legends of the X and Y axes of the grid and by the collapse/expand state of a hierarchy associated with the presentation of the dimension's name in the legend. The user can change the ordering of dimensions, expand or collapse dimensional hierarchies, or even move a dimension from one axis legend to the other, with the pivot table automatically recalculating the metrics and the row and column labels accordingly. Such capabilities can effortlessly provide multiple views into the detail data without re-creating a table for each different view. YouTube contains videos illustrating the power and ease of use of Excel pivot tables.

Many descriptive level BI tools can also provide **dashboards** and **scorecards** to present standard information and subsequently drill down. A dashboard helps monitor business and clinical activities or progress on key initiatives through highly visual representations of relatively current information, similar to gauges on an automobile dashboard. A scorecard provides a visual representation of critical business and clinical metrics. These metrics could be specific to an initiative, a business unit, or the entire organization. Scorecards may show how the metrics trend over time and how they compare to targets.

Alerts are also considered to be a type of descriptive BI by some experts. For example, the outbreak of a flu epidemic could be determined by aggregating and monitoring laboratory data across a region.

Predictive BI

At the predictive level, statistical or mathematical techniques are used to explore typically large volumes of data to discover key correlations or causal relations or to determine what might happen. Common examples of prediction include stock prices (e.g., "black box" trading), credit scoring or risk analysis (e.g., the likelihood of fraud or of defaults on payments), election results, analysis of crime patterns, the likelihood of responding to a discounted price, and sales projections. Many options exist and continue to evolve to categorize the tools and techniques used for predictive BI, such as simulations, forecasts, and predictive modeling.

For **simulations**, a model is created and used to predict results under different scenarios. Business process models created to support workflow automation can be useful in BI simulations. Another example of a simulation model in healthcare is the Archimedes Model, which claims to be "… a full-scale simulation model of human physiology, diseases, behaviors, interventions, and healthcare systems. By using advanced methods of mathematics, computing, and data systems, the Archimedes Model enables managers, researchers, administrators, and policymakers to run clinically realistic virtual trials on any population and create compelling evidence to make decisions in health and economic outcomes research, policy creation, clinical trial design, and performance improvement."[1]

Forecasting is a type of prediction that estimates a variable of interest (e.g., sales demand) at some point in the future. Forecasts may be generated by nonquantitative expert consensus, more quantitative approaches such as time series analysis of trend data, or combinations of methods. Forecasting could be used in healthcare to estimate the total number of people with diabetes or the total costs associated with a condition such as diabetes or cancer as some point in the future.

Predictive modeling is used in predictive analytics to create a statistical model of future behavior.[2] Predictive analytics is the area of data mining concerned with analyzing large volumes of data to derive meaningful business and clinical insights. These insights are typically correlations or relationships (A is related to B) rather than causality (A caused B). Implementing predictive modeling is typically a four-step process: identify the problem, explore historical data, build and validate a model, and deploy the model on new data to make predictions, ideally with probabilities of accuracy.

A variety of approaches or algorithms can be used with predictive analytics. Some of the more common include:

- Classification algorithms help predict one or more discrete variables and are frequently used to identify an "either/or" variable (e.g., the unknown variable is categorical). Examples in healthcare could include identifying characteristics of patients who do not comply with a specific therapy or classifying patients who are at high risk for a condition such as diabetes or coronary artery disease.
- Regression algorithms are used to help predict one or more continuous variables (e.g., how acuity or health status changes over time) based on correlations (not causations) with attributes in other data. For example, results of a clinical investigation may indicate a relationship between heavy coffee consumption and a higher incidence of heart attacks that is interpreted as causation, with heavy coffee drinking causing more heart attacks. Further investigation might

show that the relationship, in fact, is a correlation, with heavy coffee drinkers frequently also being heavy smokers and smoking, not coffee consumption, being the cause of a higher incidence of heart attacks.

Examples of using regression algorithms in healthcare could be developing a model to predict acute episodes of a chronic disease (e.g., diabetes or congestive heart failure) or predicting the impact that certain therapies could have on lipid or glucose values. Regression analysis first requires identifying variables that could be strongly related to the variable of interest and then developing a predictive model for the variable of interest.

- Segmentation or cluster algorithms have no variable of interest. Cluster algorithms divide data into groups or clusters of items that have similar properties. In healthcare, this technique could be used to identify subpopulations of patients within the larger population of patients (e.g., patients with coronary artery disease who have not responded to a standard course of therapy) to test new individualized treatment regimens for this subpopulation of patients. The goals of clustering[3] are to:
  - Find the variables (e.g., age, sex, income levels, health literacy, diagnostic test results, or comorbidities) that most highly influence cluster assignment
  - Compare the clusters across variables of interest
  - Assign new cases to clusters and measure the strength of cluster membership
- Association algorithms were made popular by online retailers through recommendations that "customers who bought this item also bought these items." In healthcare, such algorithms could be used to link certain types of behaviors (e.g., heavy smoking) with other types of behaviors (e.g., medication noncompliance).

A relatively recent advancement in predictive modeling is the ensemble approach, which combines the results of different models or algorithms to improve accuracy by overcoming the weaknesses of individual algorithms or models.

With advancements in computing power, results from predictive modeling are beginning to be deployed for real-time transactions in uses such as fraud detection for credit card transactions. Similar uses can be expected for monitoring real-time data in healthcare.

Prescriptive BI

The highest, most complex, and typically last level of BI to be implemented on a broad scale is prescriptive BI. Prescriptive BI is used to model a set of possible decisions to help determine the best course of action for a particular set of objectives, decision variables, and constraints. Unlike predictive BI, which helps determine what might happen, prescriptive BI helps determine the best course of action. Prescriptive BI can aid in optimizing scarce resources or choosing among different alternatives. Such optimization can be for one decision (e.g., what is the optimal care pathway for this patient being discharged that minimizes out-of-pocket charges to the patient) or for many decisions (e.g., how do we best use our post-acute care resources for all patients being discharged over the next few days).

Although prescriptive BI has not been as widely deployed in healthcare as in some other industries (e.g., to optimize scheduling or inventory levels or pricing), it offers greater longer-term potential to optimize resources or even to help provide "cognitive support" for physicians. For example, optimization approaches could be combined with other analytics tools such as data integration, data reduction, visualization, or predictive modeling to help physicians determine the best diagnostic or therapeutic approaches for patients with multiple chronic conditions.

HOW BI CAN IMPACT THE TRANSFORMATION OF HEALTHCARE

As many have noted, the current system of healthcare in the United States costs too much and does not deliver sufficiently good outcomes. Numerous market-based reforms have been or are being attempted, but they lack sufficient scope and scale to create changes on a broad level. The Affordable Care Act (ACA) has catalyzed reform efforts, setting in motion a reform initiative unlike any previous legislative attempt. The ACA promises to provide incentives to dramatically reduce the number of uninsured and is testing a number of new payment models to bend the cost curves of care delivery and wellness maintenance.

The new payment models of Medicare Shared Savings plans, ACOs, and bundled payment schemes are changing the face of reimbursement. The additional coding change to ICD-10 and its accompanying granularity and complexity creates a major challenge for most American HCOs.

The United States Congress, Centers for Medicare & Medicaid Services, and commercial purchasers have provided positive and negative incentives to which HCOs must respond to compete and prove that they can contain healthcare costs, make the population healthier, and improve quality and outcomes.

The hype of BI/analytics in 2013 has quickly become a challenging reality for HCOs. Those implementing a well-thought-out BI/analytics strategy will have a much better chance to succeed than those who perpetuate their fragmented, siloed, bolt-on environments.

Implementing an enterprise EHR and meeting the objectives of meaningful use are the first steps. HCOs now have the ability to capture structured, defined data about patient care in their acute and ambulatory environments. However, to obtain a comprehensive picture, such as determining how an HCO can avoid a readmission within 30 days, the organization still needs access to data from outside their organization, unless they own all the care sites that a patient might visit after an acute care episode. The EHR cannot provide all the information required in that scenario. Therefore, health information exchange—coupled with sophisticated BI tools that can gather data from multiple owned and non-owned systems, including claims data from payers, and housed in the organization's data warehouse—must be established to provide normalized, cleansed, structured data to clinicians and care managers who manage the patient's care before, during, and after discharge.

BI also can contribute to the growing emphasis on "population health management," which requires a broad array of analytics capabilities. In addition to requiring clean, clearly defined data from multiple owned and non-owned sources stored in a data warehouse and appropriate BI tools to use those data, the population must be risk-stratified before managing a patient's care. A taxonomy gaining popularity stratifies patients into today's high-risk and high-cost patients, rising-risk patients, and low-risk patients. Today's high-risk patients are typically relatively easy to identify using descriptive analytics. The challenge is to identify rising-risk patients using predictive analytics and appropriately intervene to prevent them from become high-risk, high-cost patients.

For low-risk members of the population, the goal is to prevent them from becoming patients. Information about their wellness can allow prediction of their use of healthcare and wellness services as well as how much money the HCO will make or lose if they do become patients. HCOs participating in ACOs cannot be successful without BI/analytics tools operating on clean, consistently defined data. Although such segmentation and identification may appear a daunting challenge, payers are typically competent at these processes because they have been performing at least parts of them for years.

Finally, prescriptive modeling can employ data from surgery, materials, billing, case management, rehabilitation, step-down care, and other systems to optimize the scheduling of employees, clinicians, patients, and materials in surgical cases.

CONCLUSION

In the near future, HCOs will undertake concerted efforts to optimize a wide variety of processes and systems as they seek to drive out unnecessary expense and make the transition from volume-based reimbursement to affordable, value-based reimbursement. As ACOs continue to form and try to capitalize on economies of scale, their need to optimize services and processes across a new "enterprise" will be essential. The ability to use advanced predictive and prescriptive modeling tools to assist in those efforts can be the difference between success and failure.

REFERENCES

1. Archimedes: Quantifying Healthcare website. www.archimedesmodel.com. Accessed December 2013.

2. Predictive modeling definition. *WhatIs.com*. http://whatis.techtarget.com/search/query?q=predictive+modeling. Accessed December 2013.

3. Cluster analysis. *StatSoft Electronic Statistics Textbook*. http://www.statsoft.com/Textbook/Statistical-Advisor/Searching-for-Clusters-or-Natural-Groups. Accessed December 2013.

CHAPTER 3

Application of Analytics to the New Healthcare Paradigms

Samuel VanNorman

In the past decades, analytics in healthcare has emerged from obscurity to become a competitive advantage for savvy organizations. In the near future, the discipline should continue to offer a competitive advantage to healthcare organizations (HCOs) willing to invest in and explore novel analytics approaches, tools and, most importantly, people. A thriving analytics program has become a requirement for all organizations. The demand for analytics both internally and externally is voracious, with the discipline moving from the sole domain of research, retrospective reporting, and single studies to an organization-wide and industry-wide demand on a near-real-time basis. Finally, the need for healthcare analytics is being driven further by standards-based approaches required by trade organizations, regulatory bodies, and vendors.

In this chapter, we explore an analogy of advancing analytics to illustrate the needs that HCOs must meet in today's changing world. We also examine the components necessary to support new healthcare paradigms, including both analytics infrastructure and information delivery.

ANALYTICS EVEREST

Consider mountaineers attempting to reach the peak of Mount Everest as a metaphor for achieving an analytics goal (Figure 3-1). The mountaineering expedition must address numerous factors to guarantee success. First, it needs a comprehensive plan before arriving at base camp. Mount Everest has multiple ascent routes, each with different needs that range from permits to travel logistics to local language. Another component of the ascent plan is a timeline addressing the highly seasonal nature of ascents, detailing the time spent at each camp along the chosen route that affords the climbers sufficient opportunity to acclimate to the altitude. The plan also evolves constantly in response to weather and environmental conditions as well as the needs of expedition members.

A successful expedition requires a mix of people with the appropriate skills. Managers handle the logistics of travel, procurement, and hiring help. Promoters recruit

Figure 3-1: Mount Everest North Face as seen from the path to the base camp, Tibet. Photo credit: Luca Galuzzi, 2006 (http://www.galuzzi.it).

appropriate mountaineers for the expedition and support staff for the ascent. The climbers themselves must possess the time, money, and skills to make the ascent. Finally, the expedition requires one or more people to guide, cajole, and even abort the ascent if necessary.

Also important is the equipment. Appropriate gear is required for climbing, accommodations at different stations on the mountain, and clothing the climbers. Food and water are needed, as is supplemental oxygen for most climbers. Depending on mountain conditions and altitude, equipment needs change as the expedition progresses, with some equipment being shed and new equipment being used, depending on the stage of the ascent.

The stakes are high in an ascent of Mount Everest. The cost of an expedition can extend into millions of dollars. Also, the potential of death is very real, be it from avalanches, exposure to weather, falls, unexpected health issues, or oxygen starvation in the death zone. Altitudes above 8,000 meters (26,000 feet) are known as the death zone. Although humans can survive for short periods at these altitudes, the body consumes more oxygen than it can take in from the atmosphere.[1]

The Everest expedition is analogous to HCOs ascending the descriptive-predictive-prescriptive analytics mountain (Figure 3-2). Many organizations remain at analytics base camp, focused on descriptive analytics. These organizations are unaware or unready for the potential of advanced applications of data, unskilled in the disciplines necessary to support advanced analytics, and unequipped with appropriate tools for the ascent.

Some organizations at base camp may attempt ascents to predictive and prescriptive analytics and retreat due to equipment (tool) failure, either using poor tools or the wrong tools, such as using report development tools for extraction, transformation, and load (ETL) or statistical analysis. Although this approach is technically possible, it is not recommended. Other organizations abort the expedition due to inadequate planning, unrealistic schedules, poor staging of projects and deliverables, lack of trans-

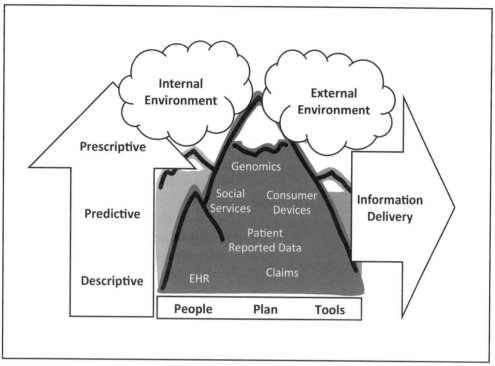

Figure 3-2: The descriptive-predictive-prescriptive analytics mountain.

parency, and insufficient funding. Some organizations remain at base camp due to assembling the wrong expedition team, assuming that capable existing teams thriving at developing reports and dashboards also can succeed with more advanced analytics projects. Finally, others are bound to base camp because of the weather; the internal and external climate may not support an advancing analytics program, despite having the right teams, tools, and plans. Savvy organizations recognize that they are at base camp, plan for the investment in people and tools, and time their expedition up the analytics mountain based on optimal internal and external environmental conditions.

Fewer organizations ascend to the predictive analytics camp. These organizations develop capability with the tools and skills required for building predictive models. Savvy organizations applying predictive analytics understand that ascension of the analytics mountain requires time for acclimation. These organizations identify additional applications to move more of the organization's focus to predictive analytics and build awareness that the journey does not end with predictive analytics.

Finally, a small number of organizations reach the analytics peak of prescriptive analytics. Combining an appropriate mix of skills and tools with timing that matches both the needs of their organization and the broader environment, these organizations tactfully apply prescriptive analytic tools to a subset of their needs. They realize that prescriptive analytics represent a powerful tool, but it is not appropriate for all situations. The organizations have also invested strategically in the tools and people required for prescriptive analytics.

As with Everest expeditions, even the most advanced organizations have a strong contingent at base camp and fewer at higher analytics altitudes. The skills and tools at different stations on the mountain may not be appropriate at all altitudes, although savvy organizations seek to maximize their investments for broadest applicability and highest value. They also have a keen eye on the environment, staying aware of new tools and changing market conditions and adapting their expeditionary plan as they progress. Finally, self-aware organizations realize that they may not be ready to tackle the Analytics Everest immediately and train on smaller mountains in preparation.

ANALYTICS INFRASTRUCTURE

The Analytics Everest encompasses a solid mountain of data. Like Mount Everest, healthcare data are frequently difficult to map, at times unstable and changing, subject to debate about best approaches, and somewhat inaccessible. Yet, underneath the surface lies a solid, stable mass of data. If the data are too unstable, the inevitable avalanche consumes any analytics program, leaving a mess in its path.

In the words of Paul Volkmuth, healthcare data warehousing pioneer, without the right analytics infrastructure, "we will be crushed under the weight of our spreadsheets and machine-assisted manual processes" (personal correspondence, 2013). This is doubly true in advanced analytics projects and programs, which frequently lend themselves to proofs of concept and prototypes.

HCOs currently struggle to maintain and manage the plethora of data created and collected during the delivery of care. For example, the 2012 release of one vendor's electronic health record (EHR) contains nearly 30,000 tables and 250,000 columns in the operational data store. Yet, the data captured and collected in the EHR represent only a subset of the information about the experience of healthcare and determinants of health. Analytically advancing organizations must address the need to access, collect, and interact with data from sources beyond their EHR (or EHRs).

CURRENT AND EMERGING DATA SOURCES

The EHR and Other Integrated Care System Applications

Data from an HCO's EHRs remain the primary source for a significant amount of analytics. However, new aspects of the data in the EHR are being accessed, including unstructured data in text fields and image data. For organizations with enterprise-wide EHRs, much of the data captured in other sources may flow to and from the EHR, providing support for care teams. Increasingly, health systems are receiving and using EHR data from other organizations, both in point-of-care delivery and analytics. The data may come from health records in similar settings of care (hospital-to-hospital, clinic-to-clinic) or disparate settings of care (home health-to-clinic, ambulance service-to-hospital, clinic-to-skilled nursing facility). Also included in this category are peripheral clinical systems integrated with the EHR, such as socioeconomic indicators from care management systems or anesthesia details from surgical systems. Much of this data has been inconsistently and incompletely integrated from an analytics perspective, omitting nuance from the patient and patient's care.

Financial Systems

Although EHRs regularly feed data to a broad variety of financial systems (e.g., billing, accounting, planning, costing), the data frequently are not reintegrated for analytic purposes. In addition to introducing issues of governance and multiple sources of truth to the analytics environment, HCOs that are not employing such reintegration are missing the value of the combined data. For example, merged financial and clinical data could provide information about the most cost-effective clinical outcomes or profile conditions and regimens at risk for reimbursement from a delivery system (rather than payer) perspective. Indiana University Health's Bloomington Hospital systematically identified 50 cost-effective pharmaceutical intervention substitutions by merging EHR and financial system data, identifying $755,000 in savings.[2]

Enterprise Master Patient Indices (EMPIs)

OpenEMPI defines the EMPI as follows:[3]

[A] repository that maintains a registry of all patients across an enterprise. An EMPI provides many benefits, including:

- Maintains a central registry of all patients and their demographics, assigning a unique identifier to each patient.
- Eliminates duplicate patient registration entries that result due to changes in patient demographics (patient moved to another location), data entry errors during patient registration, or missing demographic information.
- Provides record locator service by enabling physicians across the enterprise to identify which health care providers a patient has visited.

From an analytics perspective, an EMPI allows organizations to take a patient-centric approach to analytics. A patient-centric approach assumes that clinical events and indicators can be accurately associated with an individual patient, allowing longitudinal analysis of individuals and populations. Without a patient-centric analytics infrastructure, analyses are either more episodically focused (per an account or encounter) or at a summary level. For many HCOs with analytic programs focused primarily on data from a single EHR, the EHR implicitly serves the EMPI purpose. HCOs pursuing a patient-centric approach to integrating more complex data sources with EHR data require more complex EMPI functionality.

Claims

One of the most frequently discussed (and arguably most powerful) analytics additions to EHR data is claims data. The EHR contains a significant depth of clinical information, but it is limited to the patient's experience within a care system or even setting of care within a care system, depending on the level of EHR integration. Claims and other payer data provide a broader view of healthcare utilization, including care in other systems, pharmacy data, and home health data. However, although these data capture out-of-system utilization, they do not reflect results and specifics of care, limiting the value of claims data for some applications. Integrating claims and EHR data emphasizes the need for an EMPI strategy to reconcile patient identities between the data sets. Further complexity is introduced by a lack of consistency in data set format and level of detail, requiring normalization of the data for analyses across payers.

Patient-reported Data

HCOs collect patient-reported data through surveys on patient satisfaction and patient-reported outcomes (PROs). Although a link between patient satisfaction and clinical outcomes has not been consistently established,[4] patient satisfaction is recognized as a key component to successful healthcare delivery. Patient satisfaction is increasingly tied to both external incentives and staff compensation. Some organizations integrate satisfaction within their analytics infrastructures, but many continue to rely on stand-alone analysis of data through patient satisfaction survey vendor tools.

PROs have been collected by HCOs for primarily research purposes or focused quality improvement efforts. In either case, studies are generally time-limited and/or reserved for a sample of the total population. These data have been collected through paper surveys or interviews, generally at a significant cost. With widespread usage of electronic kiosks, patient web portals, and smartphone applications, HCOs now can administer tailored PRO surveys to a broader population without the need to sample and at a very low variable cost. These data can offer powerful insights both at the point of care and in analytics programs when derived from appropriate, validated instruments and integrated with care and analytical applications.

Consumer Devices

Much of the electronic device data available within the confines of healthcare delivery settings has been available within EHR systems and analytics systems for some time. However, the rapidly expanding "Internet of Things" that captures data relevant to healthcare offers a broad new volume and variety of data from consumer-oriented healthcare devices. The "Internet of Things," also referred to as the "Internet of Objects" and the "Internet of Everything," is a concept initially proposed by Kevin Ashton in 1999. The phrases refer to the rapidly increasing body of uniquely identifiable, Internet-accessing objects that capture and transmit data. ABI Research estimates 10 billion wirelessly connected devices in the market today, with more than 30 billion expected in 2020.[5] Data range from clinical indicators (weight, blood pressure) to activity levels to cognition.

Social Services Systems

Some healthcare delivery systems are now integrating information with social services agencies, supplementing medical data with social service utilization and other data. Despite significant legal and logistical barriers, HCOs that have succeeded in integrating social services data have realized significant value in reduced costs and improved outcomes in both social services and healthcare domains. Hennepin Health, a Medicaid program in Minnesota that combines medical, behavioral, and social services to a high-risk population, has successfully used these combined data to support interventions.[6] The result has been a greater than 20% reduction in hospital admissions and emergency department visits in the first year.

Genomics

Several academic medical systems have made significant investments in merging genomic and EHR data through data warehouses. The technology for inexpensive genomic sequencing; fast, high-capacity storage devices; and supercomputer-scale computing power have made such integration possible for analysis. The combined data offer an unprecedented ability to personalize interventions to specific patient conditions. However, as Adrian Lee, PhD, University of Pittsburgh Medical Center, noted in reference to their genomic analytics program, "We have a limitless capacity to produce data, but still a limited capacity to store, share, analyze, and use data, and that's the problem."[7]

Using the Data

The number of sources, the magnitude of data from the sources, and the volatility of the sources do not always lend themselves to traditional data management and data warehousing techniques. Although traditional data warehouses will continue to have their place, new tools and techniques, including big data applications (discussed further in Chapter 1), the logical data warehouse (LDW), and cloud-based solutions, will supplement and enhance legacy analytics systems.

The LDW has been described as "a new data management architecture for analytics which combines the strengths of traditional repository warehouses with alternative data management and access strategy. The LDW will form a new best practice by the end of 2015."[8] Essentially, the LDW combines the traditional centralized data warehouse with federation or distributed processing. The LDW provides organizations with a methodology to integrate disparate, structured sources much more quickly than full integration into a monolithic data warehouse.

"The cloud" is a nebulous term that refers to large numbers of virtual servers and storage connected to a fast network (like the Internet) that can be scaled according to demand and functionally appear to users as physical devices. Cloud applications can have a variety of manifestations. At one end of the cloud spectrum is a remote server and storage that is configured for local use within the HCO. At the other end are full-fledged remote applications and storage that appear to end users to be locally hosted, ranging from office applications to analytics suites to EHRs. Chris Hoff, Vice President of Strategy and Planning for Juniper Networks, warns, "If you suck now, you'll be pleasantly surprised by the lack of change when you move to Cloud."[9]

INFORMATION DELIVERY

Ascent of Analytics Everest is more than just a climb up the side of a mountain of data; without the ability to share the insights of the trip with a broad audience, the value of the expedition is lost. Regardless of the myriad data sources integrated and the sophisticated, clever analysis, if information is inaccessible to change agents—from executives to physicians to receptionists to patients—the investment in analytics is wasted. In *The Visual Display of Quantitative Information*, noted expert in data visualization Edward Tufte simply states, "Above all else, show the data."[10] Healthcare analytics evangelist Laura Madsen cites the necessity of sharing business intelligence (BI). Note that BI is a term that is often used interchangeably with analytics and encompasses the people, infrastructure, analysis, and presentation layers of analytics programs. Madsen notes, "[Y]our BI presentation layer will likely have many tools. Some tools are better at certain things than others, and if you have a strong analytic component to your BI program, your standard BI product will likely not meet all of your needs."[11] Forward-looking information delivery for advanced analytics has several important characteristics.

In many organizations, information delivery manifests as reports, scorecards, and dashboards, frequently with limited or no ability to manipulate or analyze data. New analyses or reports generally require specialized knowledge to develop or access and often take weeks or months to develop. Information is delivered through specialized tools outside of existing workflows and requires training to use beyond the basic level. Such limitations can result in important information not being used. These legacy tools and information delivery mechanisms may have a place, but they are insufficient to optimize outcomes, experience, and cost. In addition to new analytics sophistication, new delivery mechanisms are required in presentation layers.

A significant component of analytics is the ability to quickly derive meaning from the massive and growing quantities of data and analysis at HCOs. Although smart analysts and programming can support improved care delivery, improvements in healthcare require engagement of operational partners to build understanding and a desire for change. This can be aided with efficient, relevant distillation of data through visualization.

Data visualization is the presentation of data in graphical or pictorial format. Visualization can range from graphs and charts to maps and "infographics." Because the human brain processes images more efficiently than tables of data, data visualization tools offer increased opportunities to quickly process large amounts of data. Doing so allows individuals to uncover signals and patterns quickly, even when the volume of data is enormous. Visualizations deliver information in a commonly accepted and understandable manner, which can simplify sharing of ideas that are founded in complex data.

Visualizing healthcare data is not a new concept. In 1858, Florence Nightingale published a powerful diagram of the causes of mortality of the British army in Asia (Figure 3-3), demonstrating the magnitude of deaths from preventable illness compared to the deaths from wounds and other causes.

Successful data visualization assumes sound, relevant underlying data. In addition, thoughtful graphical design visualization serves as a filtering mechanism, eliminating or de-emphasizing less relevant information, such as only highlighting patients at high risk or clinics not meeting financial targets. One example of data visualization is how the federal government is examining large amounts of claims information to develop fraud detection tools that can visually identify "new and unusual patterns of activity."[12]

Presentation of data, whether in graphical formats or summary tables, often prompts additional questions and queries. Interactive analytics and visualizations can take many forms, from filtered spreadsheets with charts to applications specifically designed for graphical data manipulation by end users. One approach is self-service tools, which allow users to perform some analytics tasks and manipulate visualizations. Such tools are oriented toward less technically savvy users and generally require significant forethought in the development of underlying data sets and set up of the tools to provide meaningful data and support analysis. Self-service tools are becoming increasingly sophisticated, in many cases handling work previously performed by skilled developers or statisticians. For example, Beth Israel Deaconess Medical Center

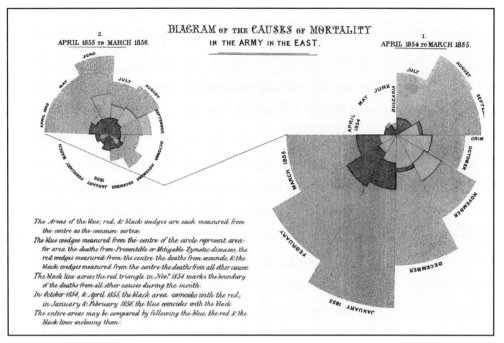

Figure 3-3: Diagram of the causes of mortality in the army in the East. Florence Nightingale created this polar area diagram in 1858.

is deploying a smartphone application with a simple user interface to allow caregivers self-service access to a 2 million-patient database with 200 million data points.[13]

Analytics programs encounter difficulty integrating tools into operational workflows. Many analytics delivery tools are increasingly easy to use by information consumers, but their adoption is reduced when the information is spread across many tools, such as separate tools or portals for clinical, quality, patient experience, and financial indicators. Integrating the data from separate sources into a single display or tool can increase usage. Also, integrating the tools within transactional systems (typically an EHR) can both increase adoption and improve efficiencies and care. A study on an EHR-integrated diabetes care dashboard found that "using a patient-specific diabetes dashboard improves both the efficiency and accuracy of acquiring data needed for high-quality diabetes care."[14] However, "if physicians had to spend too much time searching for data, they would either continue without it or order a test again."[14]

A promising and emerging area of applied healthcare analytics is point-of-care clinical decision support (CDS). CDS systems are designed to support care teams in using evidence-based medicine to make clinical decisions. Point-of-care CDS integrates tools in the examination room or next to the hospital bed, typically as part of the EHR or integrated with the EHR. Early efforts focused on prompts and alerts based on broad patient information. Newer, more sophisticated tools mine patients' EHR records to provide patient-specific recommendations grounded in patient history and other clinical data.

A 2013 study on diabetes clinical decisions support concluded, "Promising next-generation developments will include prioritizing clinical actions that have maximum benefit to a given patient at the point of care and developing effective methods to communicate CDS information to patients to better incorporate patient preferences in care decisions."[15] In some ways this is already happening. One study on patient-tailored, analytics-based CDS for pediatric obesity found that an EHR-integrated CDS program promoted higher levels of evidence-based medical care.[16] Another study demonstrated the feasibility of integrating genomic information with EHR data to provide care teams with highly tailored point-of-care decision support for gene-based prescribing.[17]

Case Study: Google.org Flu Trends

Google.org is a group within Google that leverages the organization's human and technology resources to address public interest issues. One project they have developed is an influenza tracking and prediction model based on search terms. According to their website:[18, 19]

We have found a close relationship between how many people search for flu-related topics and how many people actually have flu symptoms. Of course, not every person who searches for "flu" is actually sick, but a pattern emerges when all the flu-related search queries are added together. We compared our query counts with traditional flu surveillance systems and found that many search queries tend to be popular exactly when flu season is happening. By counting how often we see these search queries, we can estimate how much flu is circulating in different countries and regions around the world.

This work is an example of leveraging structured and unstructured data to draw novel and useful conclusions from nontraditional healthcare data sources. The Google.org model closely reflects data from the Centers for Disease Control and Prevention on a more real-time basis. The information becomes more relevant and useful when visualization tools are added to the data analysis. In Figure 3-4, the graph on the top indicates the intensity of flu levels based on the search terms for current and prior years. The map on the bottom indicates the current level of predicted flu intensity by state. The power of the visualization is further enhanced with interactivity when the user clicks on a state (or city, in an alternate view) to view predicted flu intensity at a more granular level.

Case Study: Readmission Risk Models

Readmission prediction models are an oft-mentioned application of predictive (and sometimes prescriptive) analytics. These models are designed to predict which patients are at highest risk for readmission to a hospital after being discharged, usually within a 7- or 30-day window.

Reducing readmissions represents a potentially significant impact across the Triple Aim:

- *Improved Health of the Population: Being in hospitals introduces additional health risks to patients, including hospital-acquired infections, delirium, falls, and medication errors. Appropriate avoidance of unnecessary hospital stays improves the overall health of the population.*
- *Enhanced Patient Experience of Care: From a patient perspective, inpatient hospital care can have a more significant life impact than care received in other settings. Inpatient hospital stays represent considerable burden to the patient and family, potentially involving time away from work, gaps in care for dependents, transportation issues, and financial hardship. Further, an inpatient hospital stay*

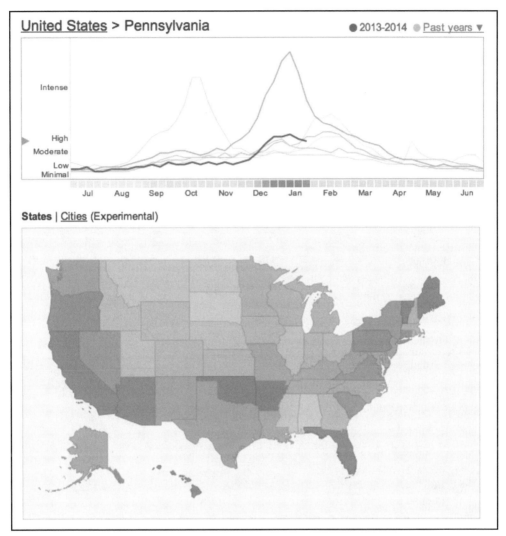

Figure 3-4: The graph on the top indicates the intensity of flu levels based on the search terms for current and prior years. The map on the bottom indicates the current level of predicted flu intensity by state. Source: Google Flu Trends (http://www.google.org/flutrends).

exposes patients to the risk of additional health issues, including infections, delirium, and other hospital-associated conditions.

- **Reduced Costs:** *The inpatient hospital bed continues to be the most costly setting for care from a payer and public health perspective, although consumers may be shielded from costs by health plan design. Historically, healthcare delivery systems have earned significant revenue from all hospital admissions, whether index admission or readmission. However, payments for readmissions are being reduced or eliminated through Medicare's Value Based Purchasing program and other total cost-of-care and pay-for-performance programs from public and private payers.*

A strong readmission model should help HCOs identify patients at high risk for readmission and aid in creation of coordinated, efficient approaches to transition from the inpatient hospital setting to lower-intensity and less-costly care environments. Despite the strong Triple Aim alignment and financial incentives, successful application of readmission prediction models has been difficult.

Vi Shaffer, Gartner Research Vice President of Healthcare, summarized one of the primary issues when she stated, "I've lost count of how many people have readmission prediction models, and some of them are pretty crummy." (Presentation at 2013 Gartner Business Intelligence and Analytics Summit, March 18, 2013.) Shaffer's evaluation is supported by the 2011 study of Kansagara and associates.[20] In this systematic review of the peer-reviewed literature on risk prediction models for hospital readmission, the authors found that "Most current readmission risk prediction models that were designed for either comparative or clinical purposes perform poorly. Although in certain settings such models may prove useful, efforts to improve their performance are needed as use becomes more widespread." Models based solely on EHR data may lack the breadth of data available from claims-based sources, while solely claims-based models may lack the depth of information available in EHR data. Further, models cannot necessarily be generalized beyond the originating institution and should be rigorously validated when applied to new settings.

A model must have moderate or strong statistical power, but a model alone is insufficient to affect readmission rates. Timeliness of the model's output is an important factor. Some commercial and organization-specific claims-based readmission (and admission) prediction models are accurate, but the models are not timely when designed around processed claims. Patients are already discharged from the hospital and may have been readmitted by the time risk data are available. The at-risk population must be identified as near to the point of index admission as possible, preferably before discharge. Organizations achieving success with risk-model–supported readmission reduction programs are profiling patients at least daily, based on EHR data that lags by 24 hours or less. Some organizations have even more aggressive programs in which they re-profile patients on a nearly real-time basis.

Output from the readmission risk model must also be actionable to care teams. Some HCOs use report, scorecard, and dashboard tools to deliver targeted information to care teams. The information can be static or interactive, integrated with the EHR, or stand-alone. Various organizations are integrating readmission risk data into the patient's EHR, manifesting through alerts, flags, banners, and custom diagnosis codes. Other HCOs pass the information directly to care teams through electronic orders, either in the EHR or other care management systems. No single method for information delivery has emerged as superior. Organizational culture and available technologies will likely drive adoption of multiple means to deliver readmission risk profiling data to care teams.

Few HCOs have made the transition from predictive to prescriptive analytics with their readmission reduction programs. Many of the current models predict readmissions based on clinical and nonclinical variables that are potentially strong for predictive purposes but cannot be addressed in the hospital setting or subsequent lower intensity care after discharge. For example, medical history, socioeconomic factors, and marital status, which are frequently statistically powerful predictors of readmissions, generally cannot be addressed by care teams unless the HCO has a strong Certified Nurse Matchmaker program.

The next generation of readmission models should progress beyond identification of at-risk populations to prescribing tailored patient- and episode-appropriate interventions and expected outcomes. Further, these new tools should seamlessly integrate into care team and patient workflows, providing tailored, timely, patient-focused care.

CONCLUSION

As HCOs ascend Analytics Everest, they need the appropriate mix of planning, people, and tools. However, no analytics program can be successful if the timing is misaligned with the needs of the organization and the broader healthcare environment. Further, as organizations advance in their analytics journey, they should constantly evaluate the mix of resources, tools, and data available in their rapidly changing environment. Also, HCOs need to build measures of success into their analytics programs beyond mere project completion. Success indicators should be real and measurable, including the voice of the customer and financial measures. Finally, HCOs must be willing to fail forward with analytics projects, terminating dead-end or irrelevant projects quickly and integrating the learning into future work.

REFERENCES

1. Wyss-Dunant E. Acclimatisation. In: Kurz M, ed. *The Mountain World*. London, United Kingdom: George Allen & Unwin Ltd; 1953:110-117.

2. Edwards R. In struggle to cut expenses, hospitals eye the pharmacy. *Hospitals and Health Networks*. 2011. http://www.hhnmag.com/hhnmag/jsp/articledisplay.jsp?dcrpath=HHNMAG/Article/data/11NOV2011/1111HHN_FEA_pharmacy&domain=HHNMAG. Accessed September 30, 2013.

3. OpenEMPI - an open enterprise master patient index. *OpenEMPI*. 2013. https://openempi.kenai.com/. Accessed September 20, 2013.

4. Fenton JJ, Jerant AF, Bertakis KD, Franks P. The cost of satisfaction: a national study of patient satisfaction, health care utilization, expenditures, and mortality. *Arch Intern Med*. 2012;172:405-411. doi: 10.1001/archinternmed.2011.1662.

5. More than 30 billion devices will wirelessly connect to the internet of everything in 2020 [press release]. London, United Kingdom: ABI Research; May 9, 2013. https://www.abiresearch.com/press/more-than-30-billion-devices-will-wirelessly-conne. Accessed December 2013.

6. Hennepin Health. Hennepin County, MN website. 2013. http://www.hennepin.us/portal/site/HennepinUS/menuitem.b1ab75471750e40fa01dfb47ccf06498/?vgnextoid=53268cee046a2310Vgn-VCM20000098fe4689RCRD. Accessed September 2013.

7. Hagland M. Leveraging IT to link genomic research and patient care in Pittsburgh. *Healthcare Informatics*. 2013. HealthcareInformatics.com: http://www.healthcare-informatics.com/article/leveraging-it-link-genomic-research-and-patient-care-pittsburgh. Accessed September 2013.

8. Blechar M. Hype cycle for information infrastructure, 2012. *Gartner*. 2012. http://www.gartner.com/id=2101415. Accessed September 2013.

9. Hoff C. *Rational Survivability*. http://www.rationalsurvivability.com/blog/. Accessed September 2013.

10. Tufte E. *The Visual Display of Quantitative Information*. Cheshire, CT: Graphics Press, LLC; 2001.

11. Madsen L. *Healthcare Business Intelligence: A Guide to Empowering Successful Data Reporting and Analytics*. Hoboken, NJ: John Wiley & Sons, Inc.; 2012.

12. Sokol L, Garcia B, Rodriguez J, West M, Johnson K. Using data mining to find fraud in HCFA health care claims. *Top Health Inf Manage.* 2001;22:1-13.

13. Eastwood B. (2013, April 23). 6 big data analytics use cases for healthcare IT. *CIO.* 2013. http://www.cio.com/article/732160/6_Big_Data_Analytics_Use_Cases_for_Healthcare_IT. Accessed September 2013.

14. Koopman RJ, Kochendorfer KM, Moore JL, et al. A diabetes dashboard and physician efficiency and accuracy in accessing data needed for high-quality diabetes care. *Ann Fam Med.* 2011;9:398-405. doi: 10.1370/afm.1286.

15. O'Connor PJ, Desai JR, Butler JC, Kharbanda EO, Sperl-Hillen JM. Current status and future prospects for electronic point-of-care clinical decision support in diabetes care. *Curr Diab Rep.* 2013;13:172-176. doi: 10.1007/s11892-012-0350-z.

16. Naureckas SM, Zweigoron R, Haverkamp KS, Kaleba EO, Pohl SJ, Ariza AJ. Developing an electronic clinical decision support system to promote guideline adherence for healthy weight management and cardiovascular risk reduction in children: a progress update. *Transl Behav Med.* 2011;1:103-107. doi: 10.1007/s13142-011-0019-1.

17. Bell GC, Crews KR, Wilkinson MR, et al. Development and use of active clinical decision support for preemptive pharmacogenomics. *J Am Med Inform Assoc.* 2013 Aug 26. doi: 10.1136/amiajnl-2013-001993. Epub ahead of print.

18. Explore flu trends – United States. *Google.org. Flu Trends.* 2013. http://www.google.org/flutrends/us/#US. Accessed September 2013.

19. How does this work? *google.org Flu Trends.* 2013. http://www.google.org/flutrends/about/how.html. Accessed September 2013.

20. Kansagara D, Englander H, Salanitro A, et al. (2011, October 11). Risk prediction models for hospital readmission: a systematic review. *JAMA.* 2011;306:1688-1698. doi:10.1001/jama.2011.1515.

CHAPTER 4

Addressing Current and Upcoming Challenges in Healthcare Analytics

Genevieve B. Melton

Future medical discoveries and breakthroughs remain uncertain yet inevitable. It is clear, however, that healthcare analytics must evolve to meet both existing and forthcoming challenges of clinical research. Generally, areas requiring evolution can be grouped broadly into: issues with data and computing, expanding end-user requirements, and specialty care needs. The complexity and magnitude of computing demands currently inhibit effective delivery of healthcare analytics, including massively parallel computing environments and ever-evolving specialized algorithms. Adoption of analytics by healthcare organizations (HCOs) and meeting the ongoing need to efficiently process large quantities of heterogeneous data for use by end users remain difficult. Providing "personalized care" through use and integration of genomic and other unique biomedical data plus the associated challenges of "unlocking" information from clinical documents represent two of the most important and complex data issues.

As outlined in other chapters, healthcare analytics must meet the needs of additional end-user stakeholders, including patients and a variety of "front-line" providers at the point of care. Finally, healthcare analytics must meet the specific needs of specialty care to provide better understanding of how best to manage patients during often costly and high-impact healthcare encounters. Processes for obtaining meaningful clinical outcomes and other clinically relevant data points, especially in specialty care, remain a bottleneck.

This chapter provides an overview of these topics, focusing on practical information to address these issues and suggest some solutions. The chapter is intended to be topical and not fully comprehensive; several important areas, including analytics related to population health and changing healthcare reimbursement models, are not covered. Further, the interesting and developing science of imaging analytics is not sufficiently mature for discussion at this time.

BIG DATA COMPUTING

A number of technologies and approaches are being used and continually improved upon to deal with the heterogeneous, complex, and large volumes of data used by healthcare and their associated computational requirements. In many cases, traditional data management and data processing approaches are insufficient. The definition of "big data" continues to evolve and is related to the needs, infrastructure, and sophistication of a given organization.[1] HCOs must understand the implications of big data without being overwhelmed by hype and marketing fears.

The framework of most big data approaches include the use of parallel or distributed storage and programming frameworks in which computing queries are split into parts and distributed to increase efficiency. Once the queries are processed, they are gathered, reassembled, and delivered. Such architectures require close management and careful analysis of the distribution of computational tasks to achieve optimal efficiencies. A programmer who writes code that does not effectively address the load or complexity of a computational task can create bottlenecks in processing and will not achieve expected efficiencies.

In addition to architectures for parallel and distributed computing, a number of technologies are becoming part of the framework, including the use of massive amounts of processors and servers (on the order of thousands) with associated memory for processing and frameworks for data storage (e.g., massively parallel-processing databases). Although the exact solution(s) for a given organization, environment, or application vary and change with time, options include highly distributed technologies with heterogeneous and geographically distributed computing solutions (e.g., grid-computing or cloud-based computing) as well as more tightly connected and protected cluster environments that allow computational resources to scale for the needs of a given organization or application. HCOs must consider a number of advantages and disadvantages of the different computing approaches and frameworks, including maintenance, expected lifespan, future needs, and local expertise. These are all highly important in determining where and how HCOs invest their time and efforts into platforms (Table 4-1). These platforms vary in the amount of coupling (the degree of dependency between computing modules) and tenancy (the number of users allocated to a set of resources within the platform).

In addition, more sophisticated computing algorithms of different types are required, as described in Chapter 5: Data Mining and Knowledge Discovery from Electronic Health Records. These include techniques from machine learning, data integration and fusion, signal processing, time series analysis, graph theory and network analysis, and decision analysis. Each of these techniques represents some of the important tools required. Because healthcare data have significant issues that make computation difficult (e.g., sparse data, missing values, and possibly questionable data accuracy), additional computational techniques are often required over traditional approaches.

Table 4-1: Primary Categories of High-Performance Computing Platforms

Large-scale Computing Platform	Computing Architectures	Advantages	Disadvantages
Cluster Computing	Multiple computers linked together that effectively function as a single computer. Typical linkage is over a local area network.	Cost-effective method; can achieve HPC; privacy issues can be addressed	Requires specialized facilities, hardware, system administrators, and IT support; less flexible
Cloud Computing	Computing that abstracts underlying hardware architectures (e.g., servers, storage, networking), enabling on-demand network access to a shared pool of computing resources that can be provisioned and released (NIST Technical Report).	Virtualization technology allows high flexibility; good for new on-the-fly HPC tasks that do not require ongoing resources	Privacy concerns; less control over processes; bottleneck may result when moving large data sets to the cloud before processing
Grid Computing	Combination of loosely coupled networked computers from different centers working together on common computational tasks. Popularized by volunteer computing efforts that "scavenge" spare computational cycles from volunteers' computers.	Ability to use large-scale computational resources at low or no cost (large-scale volunteer-based efforts)	Big data transfers are difficult; minimal control over underlying hardware, including availability and security concerns
Heterogeneous Computing	Computers that integrate specialized accelerators (e.g., GPUs or reconfigurable logic [FPGAs]) alongside GPPs.	Cluster-scale computing for a fraction of the cost of a cluster; optimized for computationally intensive fine-grained parallelism; local control of data and processes	Significant expertise and programmer time required to implement; not generally available in cluster- and cloud-based services

These platform categories are not mutually exclusive and may be combined in certain architectures.

FPGA=field-programmable gate array, GPP=general-purpose processor, GPU=graphics processing unit, HPC=high-performance computing, IT=information technology, NIST=National Institute of Standards and Technology

Adapted from Schadt et al, 2010.[1]

BIOMEDICAL DATA FOR PERSONALIZED MEDICINE

Both "patient-centered care" and "personalized medicine" seek to tailor healthcare treatments, diagnostics, and clinical protocols optimally for individual patients. At its most basic level, personalized medicine is the use of evidence and data about patients to provide treatment recommendations.[2] These ideas have been expanded upon and are often applied to electronic health record (EHR) decision-support capabilities to improve healthcare decisions at the point of care.

In its next iteration, personalized medicine integrates genetic and other biomedical information into the process of clinical decision making.[3] One approach is "pharmacogenetics," the process of identifying appropriate drug therapies by analyzing the variation in patient genomic information. An example of pharmacogenetics is the use of assays to detect responders to chemotherapy regimens for a number of solid organ and hematologic malignancies. Additional assays identify patients who are resistant to antiplatelet drugs (e.g., clopidogrel) and are at high risk of coronary thrombosis in the setting of cardiovascular disease. Related and somewhat overlapping disciplines with genomics are proteomics and metabolomics, which employ assays and computational tools to measure levels of genes, RNA, and proteins as well as the presence of certain mutations.

An important benchmark within genomics that is often cited for heralding the era of "mainstream" personalized medicine is the substantially decreased cost of DNA sequencing. As shown in Figure 4-1, the cost of DNA sequencing of a human-sized genome (grey diamonds) has outpaced "Moore's Law" (white line) greatly.[4] Moore's Law[5] is an observation coined in the context of computer hardware that has been applied to the advancement of other technologies. Moore's observation was that the cost and

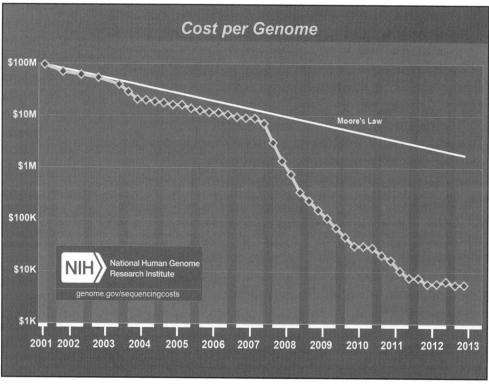

Figure 4-1: Cost for genome sequencing. Vertical axis is a logarithmic scale of cost, horizontal axis is year, squares=cost per human-sized genome, white line=theoretical plot of Moore's Law.[4]

"computing power" roughly doubles every 2 years. Generally, areas of technology that keep pace with Moore's Law are considered to be performing remarkably well. Starting in 2008, with the adoption of second-generation Sanger-based DNA sequencing, costs of DNA sequencing dropped precipitously and have well outpaced Moore's Law. This has increased the practical accessibility of genomic information but also creates the further challenges and costs of data storage and maintenance for the primary data and the associated secondary summary information.

In addition to the deluge of data from genomics, some of the greater downstream implications of personalized medicine include the need for additional tools and techniques to synthesize data into knowledge, with the ultimate goal of deriving clinically actionable information. Even within biomedical research, the trend is increasingly shifting from genomic medicine toward systems biology in an effort to understand more complex processes at a disease and organism level. Such understanding assists in weighing treatments and other clinical decisions in the context of efficacy, cost, and patient preferences (Figure 4-2).

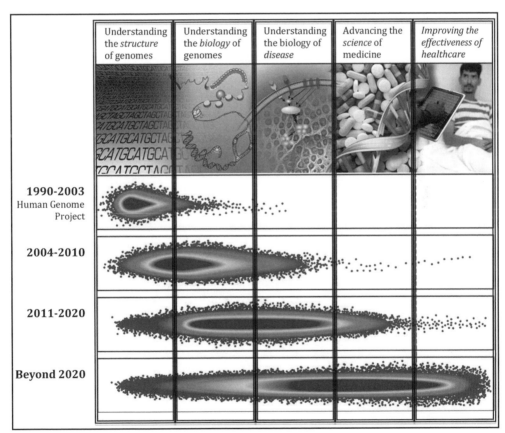

Figure 4-2: Research trends advancing the science of medicine and delivery of healthcare.[6] Each dot is suggestive of a research contribution. Later years demonstrate greater density of contributions extending further "to the right," focusing on healthcare effectiveness. (Reprinted with permission from *Nature Reviews Genetics*; 2011)

Because of these changes, expertise in bioinformatics and translational informatics are becoming increasingly important. The ability to curate, transform, reuse, and synthesize associated information requires changes to current EHR decision support systems, greater sophistication of clinicians, and increased capacity to provide secondary use and other analytics of this information. Moreover, because of the relatively higher cost of these technologies and developments, HCOs need to implement strategies to determine the necessary investment for each technology, including associated equipment, computing infrastructure, and education.

NATURAL LANGUAGE PROCESSING: UNLOCKING INFORMATION FROM CLINICAL TEXT

Many medical documents, such as discharge summaries, operative reports, and radiology reports, contain large quantities of patient information represented as findings, signs and symptoms, and diseases that can be used for a wide range of secondary applications. Both clinical text mining and natural language processing (NLP) seek to provide automated use and extraction of information from clinical text. Text mining and natural language processing were originally established as cross-disciplinary fields based in the area of artificial intelligence within computer science and computational linguistics.[7] In most cases, these techniques were developed using widely available documents or "corpora" (bodies of text) such as the print news media (e.g., *Wall Street Journal* corpora) and biomedical literature (e.g., GENIA corpus[8]).

The application of these technologies to clinical documents is relatively immature as a discipline, and certain challenges remain in their effective use. For example, clinical documents are not structured formally like formal written documents from general English or the biomedical literature, which form the basis of existing NLP software. Clinical documents also tend to have a significant number of differences in language from one document to another, referred to as a sublanguage. As an example, the structure, content, and language used in a cardiology admission history and physical examination tends to vary significantly from that of a breast surgery operative note. For this reason, NLP tools often must be customized to achieve good performance from NLP software.

Because providers have limited time to enter clinical notes, statements frequently contain grammatically poor language, medical-specific abbreviations, omission of important information, negation, uncertainty, and misspellings or incorrect word usage.[9] As a result, existing NLP software developed with general English or even the biomedical literature may not perform well for medical text. Moreover, domain terminologies and local dialects are prevalent in medical documents. For example, physicians at different hospital sites often develop their own local jargon for devices, techniques, or other items.

Documents contain large numbers of described findings and diseases. Of these, about half typically are absent or questionable in a given patient, as illustrated by the following two statements: "The patient denies any abnormal behaviors, movements, or rash anywhere else on his body..." and "Unlikely diagnosis of DIC...". The first statement contains negation and the second has uncertainty. Furthermore, the second statement contains an acronym that requires proper word sense disambiguation for the computer to process the statement properly (i.e., DIC is an abbreviation for disseminated intravascular coagulation). Therefore, negation detection and uncertainty detection are critical components in medical NLP systems. In medical text, negation detection may not be easy because negation can be explicit (e.g., "Patient denies any fevers, emesis, or diarrhea.") or implicit (e.g., "Chest x-ray is clear upon my read.").

Because the exact application of a particular NLP system is not always known, the typical approach to storing the results of these systems is to maintain the processed text with the associated data with "marked-up" text, using extensible markup language (XML) or similar markup language to maintain a wide range of mappings for text in a given document. Processing the document requires the most time and processing power, which makes retrieval of information from the marked-up text efficient (sometimes called information extraction). On the other hand, storage costs are inherent with processing documents up-front. Depending upon the amount of information encoded, document sizes can increase by several orders of magnitude. Similar to the challenges of genomic information, but to a lesser extent, this has implications for the architecture of an organization's analytics infrastructure.

Complementary to NLP in the generation of clinical documents is the use of templates and synoptic reporting at the point of care as documentation is being generated. Synoptic reports create documentation in a format with discrete data fields where each piece of desired information for a given document has a specific format. In contrast, templated documents have a variety of formats, ranging from nearly free text with a moderately structured overall format to a presentation that is very similar to synoptic reports. Synoptic reports have been used extensively in the field of pathology to collect information for secondary uses such as tumor registries.[10] They have been proposed as a means to collect important information from operative reports and other clinical documents that can improve the performance of automated text-mining systems. Synoptic reporting appears to be a successful paradigm for pathology, but its use is not yet widespread in other care areas, although it does represent an opportunity to capture data better at the point of care.

Despite these challenges, technologies to better use clinical text for healthcare analytics applications carry substantial potential for gaining additional meaningful information about patients. Some successful application areas of NLP include the detection of adverse events, automated diagnosis to assist coders, detection of clinically significant outcomes, and use of NLP within decision support systems to identify patients with significant changes in medical status. Ultimately, as they improve, clinical NLP system technologies should be able to deal with the variability and complexity of written medical language in clinical documents to provide information for secondary analysis. Because the richness of information within clinical texts and the value of communication between clinicians through documentation remain a mainstay of patient care, improvement and wider use of these techniques for healthcare analytics applications very likely will be increasingly important.

EXPANDING HEALTHCARE ANALYTICS CAPABILITIES FOR SPECIALTY CARE

A central paradigm for successful healthcare analytics is the need for actionable data for end users to make better decisions surrounding investment of resources, care models, and other clinical decision making. However, one of the greatest remaining challenges for healthcare analytics is creating usable information for specialty care. This includes the need to gain efficiencies for highly complex patients undergoing costly treatments and the associated effort currently required to obtain clinically relevant data points, especially specialty-specific clinical outcomes, at a low cost.

In many medical specialties, clinical registries have become the exemplar for obtaining quality clinical data and, in turn, are used for quality improvement for specialty care. With little exception, however, these registries require significant manual labor and cost that create a barrier to their mainstream and widespread use. In places where registries are implemented, their integration into the HCO's analytics framework is paramount to provide decision makers and administrators with a rational approach to using resources most wisely. However, without improvements to make clinical registries more affordable to HCOs, including potential changes in clinician workflow or augmentation of technologies to automatically populate registries, the collection of highly granular and accurate clinical data points will remain an area of significant challenge.

The American College of Surgeons National Surgical Quality Improvement Project (NSQIP) is an exemplar of a high-quality surgical outcomes registry.[11] Because data are collected with the goal of clinical accuracy, the NSQIP has credibility with surgical leaders and researchers, which is a critical factor for its use and value. Unfortunately, substantial resources are required by hospitals to deploy and use NSQIP, rendering its market penetration to only approximately 500 centers nationally and limited dissemination beyond tertiary medical centers. Data collection practices primarily rely upon labor-intensive and costly abstraction of medical records. It is so labor intense, in fact, that cases are sampled at most centers because collecting data on the outcomes of all surgeries is cost prohibitive. However, compared with other data collection methodologies, including information from claims or other clinical data proxies (such as laboratory values), registry data such as that provided by NSQIP are perhaps the richest and most credible data for providers and healthcare decision makers. The balance of data cost and accuracy will continue for the near future to be an important factor for those who are critically examining specialty outcomes to pinpoint approaches to further improve care, particularly for leaders of HCOs and other sponsors and stakeholders in this work.

In addition to the issues of registry data collection and integration (the latter of which is not addressed here), specialty care requires significantly detailed information on a relatively small group of patients or often the need to understand patients receiving multidisciplinary care with multiple caregivers in highly complex patient care scenarios.[12] In these cases, clinical care pathways and pattern recognition are important to place patients into various treatment paradigms and pathways. Moreover, low-volume centers may realize value in pooling data from multiple centers to benchmark and understand variability in specialty care. Ultimately, until there are more efficient methods to collect clinical data for specialty care as well as more facile methods to model complex and changing care pathways, healthcare administrators with specialty care should focus upon areas within their organization that have significant volume and cost variability when developing specialty-specific analytics platforms.

TAILORING AND DELIVERING ANALYTIC RESULTS FOR OTHER HEALTHCARE STAKEHOLDERS

The traditional consumers of healthcare analytics include administrative leaders, managers, quality improvement personnel, and clinician champions who are responsible for managing and improving the performance of HCOs. Today, end users such as physicians, nurses, or other care providers require actionable data tailored for their context. Ultimately, patient consumers will have greater choice in their care and access to organizational outcome data. Whether consumers get this information through governmental and regulatory sources or directly from HCOs (i.e., as market differentiators), resources for consumers should become an area of increasing importance in healthcare analytics.

Tailoring data provided to those at the front line of care for comparisons is critical. Examples include comparing the user to other peers, those in similar practice settings and roles, and those within their specialty area. Many HCOs currently provide simple reports or even dashboards, but the next generation of analytic delivery solutions for clinicians will have more sophisticated capabilities. For example, placing actionable data at the point of care into the workflow will be essential to making its use and incorporation into decision making as seamless as possible.

Other important capabilities include the provision of patient-specific information synthesized to compare to similar patient populations or tailored to the care setting and context of the clinician (e.g., information provided in the acute inpatient setting to a specialty provider compared to information provided to a care coordinator in the primary care ambulatory setting should be different for the same patient). The data also should provide relevant clinical evidence to clinicians, which represents one of the greater challenges for analytics platforms in the goal of achieving high-quality, low-cost clinical care.

As biomedical and clinical discoveries and understanding of the best care for patients accelerate, clinicians, healthcare systems, and even clinical authorities are having increasing difficulty keeping up with current evidence and updating their practices based on recommendations of decision support systems, clinical protocols, and analytics platforms. To meet this challenge, additional tools are needed to provide not only patient-specific data but also current and synthesized evidence for making effective decisions. This area requires significant maintenance because rules about using clinical data change and evolve with time, including decision support rules and algorithms for prescriptive healthcare decision making.

Healthcare analytics delivery to patient consumers is nascent in its overall development. Patients have several resources to obtain publically reported data about institutions, such as Hospital Compare[13] and magazines that synthesize HCO performance data (e.g., *US News & World Report* and *Consumer Reports*). With the growth of health insurance exchanges and other market differentiators, consumers will desire and eventually expect deeper and greater information delivered directly to them. As part of meaningful use and other national initiatives to improve patient engagement in healthcare, personal health records have become the first step for patients to access their healthcare data. HCOs that can effectively provide patient consumers with deeper *yet understandable* information about their health status, outcomes, and the safety and quality of their care will likely have a market advantage in the future.

CONCLUSIONS

The next generation of healthcare analytics must address a number of current and future challenges, each of which is substantial and has exciting potential for development. Advances in healthcare computing and techniques to address the era of big data focus on the advent of personalized medicine and unlock phenotypic and clinically important information from clinical documents with NLP hold great promise for healthcare analytics. Meeting the data and information needs of specialty care, front-line clinicians, and ultimately patient consumers presents one of the greatest challenges and opportunities. These and other unanticipated future developments will be important parts of future iterations of healthcare analytics.

REFERENCES

1. Schadt EE, Linderman MD, Sorenson J, Lee L, Nolan GP. Computational solutions to large-scale data management and analysis. Nat Rev Genet. 2010;11:647-657. doi: 10.1038/nrg2857.

2. Goldberger JJ, Buxton AE. Personalized medicine vs guideline-based medicine. *JAMA*. 2013;309:2559-2560. doi: 10.1001/jama.2013.6629.

3. Chute CG, Kohane IS. Genomic medicine, health information technology, and patient care. *JAMA*. 2013;309:1467-1468. doi: 10.1001/jama.2013.1414.

4. Wetterstrand K. DNA sequencing costs: data from the NHGRI Genome Sequencing Program (GSP). *National Human Genome Research Institute*. 2013. http://www.genome.gov/sequencingcosts. Accessed September 2013.

5. Moore GE. Cramming more components onto integrated circuits. *Electronics*. 1965;38:4-8.

6. Green ED, Guyer MS; National Human Genome Research Institute. Charting a course for genomic medicine from base pairs to bedside. *Nature*. 2011;470:204-213. doi: 10.1038/nature09764.

7. Jurafsky D, Martin JH. *Speech and Language Processing*. 2nd ed. Upper Saddle River, NJ: Pearson Prentice Hall; 2008.

8. GENIA corpus. *Advanced Natural Langue Process and Text Mining Technnology*. Tokyo, Japan: Tsujii Laboratory. http://www.nactem.ac.uk/aNT/genia.html. Accessed September 2013.

9. Nadkarni PM, Ohno-Machado L, Chapman WW. Natural language processing: an introduction. *J Am Med Inform Assoc*. 2011;18:544-551. doi: 10.1136/amiajnl-2011-000464.

10. Hassell LA, Parwani AV, Weiss L, Jones MA, Ye J. Challenges and opportunities in the adoption of College of American Pathologists checklists in electronic format: perspectives and experience of Reporting Pathology Protocols Project (RPP2) participant laboratories. *Arch Pathol Lab Med*. 2010;134:1152-1159. doi: 10.1043/2009-0386-OA.1.

11. Hall BL, Hamilton BH, Richards K, Bilimoria KY, Cohen ME, Ko CY. Does surgical quality improve in the American College of Surgeons National Surgical Quality Improvement Program: an evaluation of all participating hospitals. *Ann Surg*. 2009;250:363-376. doi: 10.1097/SLA.0b013e3181b4148f.

12. Bollyky TJ, Cockburn IM, Berndt E. Bridging the gap: improving clinical development and the regulatory pathways for health products for neglected diseases. *Clin Trials*. 2010;7:719-734. doi: 10.1177/1740774510386390.

13. *Hospital Compare*. Medicare.gov. 2013. http://www.medicare.gov/hospitalcompare/search.html. Accessed September 2013.

CHAPTER 5

Data Mining and Knowledge Discovery from Electronic Health Records

György J. Simon

The widespread use and continuing adaptation of electronic health records (EHRs) in healthcare has created an unparalleled opportunity to discover new medical knowledge. The range of this knowledge is unprecedented, encompassing treatment effectiveness, detailed patient population stratification, and causes of diseases, all which can lead to more personalized treatment. Data mining on top of EHR systems can help to end the "one-model-fits-all" treatment paradigm. These data can aid in tailoring treatment to the specific characteristics of the target patient, creating personalized medicine in the near future.

However, use of EHR systems has inherent challenges that must be investigated thoroughly and addressed carefully before the healthcare industry can unlock the full potential of the personalized medicine paradigm. EHR systems were designed to simplify the documentation of care and its related processes; they were not intended as the important research platform they are rapidly becoming. Research performed on top of an EHR is referred to as secondary use of the EHR data. Some of the technical challenges of secondary use can be easily overcome, but others relating to the partial observability of the data present are not so easily addressed. In this chapter, we briefly review of the challenges presented by the secondary use of EHR data and describe three related applications that highlight the opportunities for discovering interesting knowledge from such data.

CHALLENGES WITH SECONDARY USE OF EHR DATA

Let us illustrate the challenges with a hypothetical EHR system and case study. The hypothetical EHR system is composed of several subsystems, including (medication) orders, laboratory results, diagnoses, vital signs and measures, demographics, and potentially a subsystem for tracking the patient's history. In reality, these systems can be arbitrarily complex, but in this example we simplify the presentation to the most relevant subsystems for the case study.

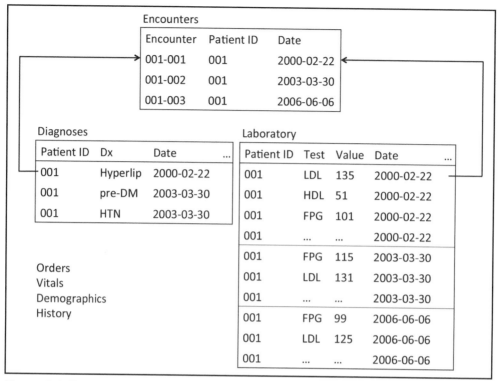

Figure 5-1: Data for the case study in the hypothetical EHR system. Information pertinent to a particular encounter (patient visit) is scattered across multiple tables and needs to be linked for analytics.

Figure 5-1 depicts the patient's records at the time of three visits. During the first visit in 2000, the patient is overweight, and a cholesterol panel reveals high low-density lipoprotein (LDL) cholesterol values. The patient admits to having had high cholesterol before and is prescribed statins. The provider notes that he refers the patient to lifestyle change consultation. The next patient encounter is seen in 2003, when he presents with elevated fasting plasma glucose (FPG) values and is tentatively diagnosed with pre-diabetes. He also has high blood pressure and is prescribed angiotensin-converting enzyme (ACE) inhibitors. Once again, he is referred to lifestyle change consultation. During his third visit in 2006, his blood pressure, FPG, and LDL cholesterol values are within normal ranges. At present, we have no further information about this patient.

Partial View of the Patient's Trajectory

From both an analytics and clinical perspective, the most obvious challenge presented in this case is the lack of information before 2003. Some of this information may be present in the clinical notes (e.g., patient admitted having had high cholesterol values before), but such data can be inaccurate and incomplete (e.g., which cholesterol measurement was high and how high). The patient's overweight status may be visible during the visit and can be quantified through the body mass index (BMI), but the duration of this condition is unknown. Unavailability of information before a certain time point (e.g., 2003) is termed "left censoring." Statistical techniques can use partial information

PID	Date	Gender	...	Hyperlip	preDM	HTN	...	LDL	FPG	HDL	ALB	CRT	...
001	2000-02-22	M	...	Y			...	135	101	51			...
001	2003-03-30	M	...		Y	Y	...	131	115	54			...
001	2006-06-06	M	...				...	125	99	55			...

Figure 5-2: Encounters of the hypothetical patient in a de-normalized analytics table in which most of the fields are missing.

from left-censored data, but the ability to reconstruct the patient's history accurately and completely is compromised.

Table De-normalization

Information for patients typically is scattered across multiple subsystems. Even a clinical data repository, which standardizes patient data from disparate sources into a cohesive format in a data warehouse, comprises numerous tables, each offering a partial view of patient information.

Distributing data into multiple topical tables is termed "data normalization" and offers important benefits, including storage efficiency, reduced data redundancy, and creation of explicit connections among the data elements. For analysis, however, data need to be de-normalized, with every record for the patient linked and transformed into a single analysis table. Currently existing statistical and data mining techniques operate on a single table (a data matrix in mathematical terminology) whose columns correspond to the individual variables, such as one column for each diagnosis code, each medication, and each laboratory result. Many techniques require the rows to represent patients, while more advanced methods allow for rows to represent encounters (Figure 5-2).

Missing Data

Analytics practitioners tend to think of data tables as primarily filled, with few elements missing, but in the case study analysis table, most of the data are missing. Some data are erroneously missing (e.g., a laboratory test was performed, but the record is lost), and other data are structurally missing (e.g., the test was not performed during the encounter). Many techniques can address erroneously missing data, but structurally missing data pose a serious challenge because such missing data contain useful information. This concept can be illustrated by a retrospective diabetes study in which some of the study participants are healthy 22-year-old people with normal glucose values. Such patients have no glucose tolerance data (structurally missing), which reflects the provider's opinion that the particular patient is very unlikely to have diabetes.

Aggregating Detailed Data

Hierarchies (ontologies) exist for many data elements, such as diagnosis codes and medications. These ontologies describe relationships. For example the International Statistical Classification of Diseases, 9th revision (ICD-9) CT code 250.02 is "uncontrolled diabetes with ketoacidosis" (Clinical Classification Software [CCS] category

3.3.1) that is categorized under "diabetes mellitus with complications" (CCS category 3.3), an "endocrine, nutritional and metabolic disorder" (CCS category 3). Similar ontologies exist for medications.

In the EHR, diagnoses and medications are recorded at the most detailed level. Depending on the clinical question, differences between two detailed codes may be irrelevant. In such cases, aggregating the individual ICD-9 codes to higher-level codes can increase the statistical power of the analysis.

Fragmentation

Data fragmentation occurs when a patient receives treatment from multiple providers who do not share clinical data. For example, a patient may go to the nearest emergency department for asthma exacerbations but may receive his regular treatment from a specialty clinic. Neither the specialty clinic nor the emergency department has a complete view of the patient's history and trajectory.

New Diagnosis Codes and Changing Diagnosis Definitions

Data mining studies are often retrospective and, therefore, affected by the introduction of new diagnosis codes or changes in diagnostic criteria. For example, the diagnostic criterion for diabetes changed from a glucose value of 7.8 mmol/L to a value of 7.0 mmol/L in 1997. To provide consistent results, the analysis must take such changes into account.

Unobservable Determinants of Outcomes

Based on the data contained in the hypothetical EHR system, the patient in the case study could be a data point in a study of the effect of ACE inhibitors in patients who do not take aspirin. However, two caveats must be addressed for the patient to be considered for the study. First, the orders subsystem does not allow investigators to determine whether the patient is taking aspirin over-the-counter (although the clinical notes may provide some guidance). Second, data are not available to explain whether the improvement in the patient's blood pressure, which returned to normal by 2006, was due to the ACE inhibitor therapy or lifestyle changes that the patient finally decided to implement in 2003 after repeated consultations.

OPPORTUNITIES FOR DATA MINING

The fundamental question that data mining might answer is which patients will benefit the most from which intervention. This question, in turn, raises a number of related questions:

- Are there patient subpopulations that behave differently from the general population? Certain patients may be at significantly increased (or decreased) risk of an outcome or respond to interventions differently, potentially requiring more or different interventions.
- What is the effect of interventions in each subpopulation? The answers to this question may allow clinicians to identify interventions that work particularly well in certain subpopulations.

The following case studies highlight opportunities that mining EHR data can offer. All three studies are related to diabetes, are from the Mayo Clinic, and build on each other. The first is a phenotype extraction study, in which we identify patients who have type 2 diabetes mellitus (T2DM) based solely on EHR data. This study directly addresses the challenges that EHRs pose. The ability to identify patients presenting with a particular condition without solely relying on the diagnosis codes protects against changing criteria of diagnoses and the lack of diagnosis codes for particular conditions. In addition, to some degree, this ability allows reconstruction of patient histories and bypasses the effects of left censoring.

Once the patient histories have been reconstructed, the second study demonstrates how to build a new subpopulation-based diabetes index. The goal is to construct a diabetes index that is more accurate than the currently existing ones by including interactions among various conditions.

The third study illustrates the effect of different interventions in various subpopulations. Specifically, we quantify the effect of statins in various pre-diabetic subpopulations.

Case Study 1. Type 2 Diabetes Mellitus Phenotype Extraction

The aim of the first case study is to identify patients with T2DM. However, rather than producing results that are directly applicable in clinical practice, the study lays the foundation for mining patterns from EHRs. Many challenges associated with using EHRs revolve around the ability to observe patient histories only partially (left censoring and fragmentation), necessitating a method for completing patient histories. As noted previously, changes in diagnostic criteria and preferred laboratory tests as well as introduction of new diagnostic codes affect the ability to identify patients in EHRs based solely on diagnostic codes.

One approach to overcoming this challenge is to use phenotyping algorithms to "diagnose" patients (or backfill their medical histories) in a consistent manner. Such algorithms ensure that patients with a particular history are held to the same standard of diagnosis.

Phenotyping algorithms are expert-crafted or machine-learned algorithms—typically, a collection of rules—that can automatically identify patients who adhere to a particular predefined study protocol or present with a particular condition based on evidence that can be "seen." Several nationwide studies have demonstrated that secondary use of EHR data can support patient identification through phenotyping algorithms. An example of phenotyping algorithms is the eMerge algorithm for T2DM: www.phekb.org/phenotype/type-2-diabetes-mellitus. Expert-created phenotyping algorithms are created through the laborious process of iterative refinement, where experts repeatedly refine rules until the resulting algorithm has high accuracy. Although these algorithms have been shown to have high accuracy, they are only available for common conditions because of the effort that their development requires. Developing them for all conditions is currently prohibitively expensive.

This is a gap that data mining can fill. Reviewing the EHRs for known cases and controls, data mining techniques can be used to construct machine-learned phenotyping algorithms, which offer performance comparable to the expert-crafted algorithms. As an illustration, in this study, we used data mining to construct a T2DM algorithm. Table 5-1 presents the rules that have higher precision than the diagnosis codes alone.

Table 5-1: Automatically Constructed Phenotype Definitions for Type 2 Diabetes Mellitus*

Number of Patients	Number of Cases of Type 2 Diabetes Mellitus	Precision	Conditions
281	270	.961	Diabetes mellitus without complications, hypertension with complications, acute renal failure, and abnormal glycated hemoglobin (HbA1c)
280	269	.960	Diabetes mellitus without complications, anemia, retinopathy, abnormal HbA1c
274	263	.950	Diabetes mellitus without complications, gout, anemia, retinopathy, screening for suspected condition, abnormal HbA1c
278	263	.940	Diabetes mellitus without complications, gout, anemia, abnormal HbA1c
278	263	.940	Diabetes mellitus without complications, anemia, hypertension, fractures, open wounds, abnormal HbA1c

* For brevity, only the five most precise definitions (rules) are displayed. They provide higher precision than the corresponding diabetes diagnosis codes alone.

The first rule states that patients who have diabetes mellitus, hypertension, acute renal failure, and abnormal glycated hemoglobin (HbA1c) values likely have T2DM. Among 281 patients with these conditions, 270 (96.1%) had a T2DM diagnosis. The key to the success for these algorithms is that they can incorporate a number of findings that are associated with diabetes, including comorbid conditions (hypertension), consequences (renal disease), and the current definition of the disease (abnormal HbA1c). This property leads us to believe that machine-learned phenotyping algorithms can be used to backfill patient histories reliably, which enables the analyses described in the subsequent case studies.

Case Study 2. Pre-diabetes Subtype Identification

A well-designed diabetes index can be a useful tool in clinical practice, potentially guiding physicians toward more optimal treatment of patients, reducing costs, and improving outcomes. In an attempt to fulfill this potential, a large number of diabetes indices have been developed, each exceeding the previous one in accuracy and specialization. Despite substantial effort, however, few indices have found acceptance in practice. The exception is the Framingham diabetes score, which stands apart from the rest and is actively used in practice.

The popularity of the Framingham score stems from the simplicity of its application. The risk factors it employs are simple to obtain. The key factors are age, blood pressure, cholesterol and glucose values, and family history of diabetes. This stands in stark contrast to some other indices that may be more accurate but require hard-to-obtain risk factors such as caloric intake from red meat. In addition, the Framingham score can be easily computed using paper and pencil. For each risk factor, the patient receives a predetermined score if the risk factor is present, and the final score is simply the sum of the scores of the individual risk factors. Patients with high final scores are treated more aggressively, while those with lower scores are treated less aggressively.

The Framingham score and other currently existing diabetes indices have two key shortcomings. First, they are additive, with each risk factor increasing the risk score by a predetermined amount independently of the other risk factors. Such an index inherently overlooks important details. For example, there is a difference in risk between patients who have high blood pressure and do not take medications and those who have high blood pressure despite taking antihypertensive drugs. Such a difference cannot be expressed in an additive mathematical form. Even more importantly, the existing indices follow the "one-model-fits-all-patients" paradigm in which the entire patient population, despite containing diverse elements, is described by a single model. This is particularly important with diabetes, a highly heterogeneous disease with potentially multiple subtypes. Each subtype and the corresponding patient subpopulation can have different risk factors, different outcomes, and different responses to interventions.

Our goal with this study was to develop a new diabetes index that has increased accuracy and information content based on risk factors that are commonly available from an EHR system. We attempted to design a diabetes index relating to the concept of diabetes subpopulations and their expected risks and response to treatment. Specifically, we considered a pre-diabetic subpopulation based on the Rochester Epidemiology Project (REP) cohort, which consists of all residents of Olmstead County in Minnesota, who are followed throughout their residence in that county. Olmstead County has few medical providers, with the two major providers sharing clinical information for research purposes. Such sharing alleviates data fragmentation problems because almost all encounters with patients are documented.

The risk factors we chose were conditions and diagnoses (obesity, hyperlipidemia, hypertension, and various cardiac and vascular diseases), related abnormal laboratory results, vital signs, medications, and patient demographic information extracted from the EHR.

We attempted to identify patient subpopulations characterized by a set of shared risk factors that indicate increased risk of progression from pre-diabetes to overt diabetes. To quantify patient risk correctly, we must adjust for age, sex, and duration of follow-up. To this end, we applied Cox proportional hazard models and computed the patients' residual risk of developing diabetes, that is, the risk that cannot be explained by age, sex, and follow-up time (conditions that cannot be modified) but can potentially be explained by comorbid conditions (information that can be incorporated into clinical care and acted upon). We developed a novel data mining technique of distributional association rule mining to associate patients' comorbid conditions with significantly elevated (or reduced) residual risk of diabetes. The result of the mining process is a collection of association rules, each comprising a set of comorbid conditions (e.g., obese, hypertension) and the associated relative risk (1.78 for these conditions). The rule means that patients who are obese and hypertensive have a 1.78 times higher risk than patients of the same age, sex, and follow-up who are either not hypertensive or not obese (or do not have any of these conditions).

In our initial study, we considered eight conditions: obesity (OB), hypertension (HTN), hyperlipidemia (HL), ischemic heart disease (IHD), cardiovascular disease (CVD),

Table 5-2: Significant Association Rules

Number of Patients	Number of Cases of Diabetes Within Subpopulation	Statistical Significance (P Value)	Relative Risk	Rule
7,116	819	2.0e-7	1.32	HTN
4,729	560	1.7e-8	1.45	OB
8,612	964	2.6e-8	1.31	HL
1,980	291	1.9e-9	1.78	HTN, OB
4,171	534	1.5e-8	1.47	HTN, HL
553	85	8.3e-4	1.86	OB, IHD
2,434	335	4.3e-9	1.68	OB, HL
382	66	7.7e-4	2.08	HTN, OB, IHD
1,271	204	2.8e-8	1.93	HTN, OB, HL
470	76	7.2e-4	1.93	OB, IHD, HL
339	61	6.1e-4	2.15	HTN, OB, IHD, HL

carotid disease, peripheral vascular disease (PVD), and renal failure. These conditions were included in the analysis if they occurred before the diabetes diagnosis. We found 11 significant rules (Table 5-2).

The rules are clinically relevant and the relative risk estimates are in line with expectations. As patients have increasing numbers of comorbid conditions, the risk of diabetes increases. An additional product of these rules is a progression graph that depicts how patient groups progress from a healthy state toward overt diabetes (Figure 5-3).

According to the graph, hypertension confers a relative risk of developing diabetes of 1.32 on the 7,116 patients who present with this condition. As the cohort acquires obesity (1,980 such patients) the relative risk increases to 1.78. When they acquire hyperlipidemia (1,271 such patients), their risk increases to 1.93. Finally, 339 patients develop ischemic heart disease added to the previous three conditions, and their relative risk of diabetes is 2.15.

Theoretically, several thousand such progression patterns can be constructed with the eight conditions included in the preliminary data set. Even limiting the data to four conditions could result in construction of 24 progression patterns. However, only 11 patterns appeared in the data set, suggesting that patients do not acquire comorbid conditions at random. Rather, comorbidities are acquired along a relatively small number of patterns.

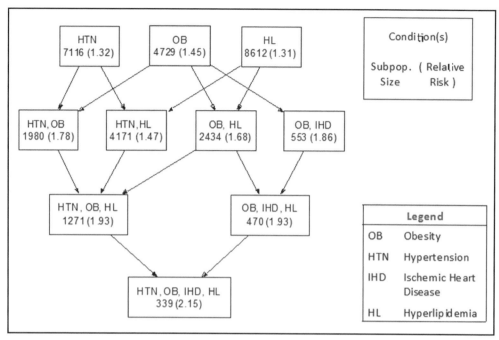

Figure 5-3: Patterns through which subpopulations progress from a healthy state toward diabetes. Each box represents a subpopulation characterized by the conditions that the corresponding patients have. The box also presents the number of affected patients as well as their age, sex, and follow-up adjusted relative risk (in parenthesis). As patients accumulate comorbid conditions, their risk increases.

The progression graph raises a number of important clinical questions that we currently are investigating. One question is whether the graph is completely predetermined or whether progression can be influenced with interventions. If such influence could be exerted, clinicians could treat patients so as to avoid states of particularly high risk. Another question is which arrows (transitions between states) are reversible. Reversible arrows can become therapeutic targets.

Preliminary study with only the eight cited conditions has yielded promising and interesting results. We have also conducted a study on the full set of diagnosis codes, medications, abnormal laboratory results, and vital signs.

Case Study 3. Effect of Statins in Pre-diabetes Subtypes

Currently, reports on the effects of statins have yielded confusing results, which have been highlighted in the 2013 editorial of the British Medical Journal. *Statins are known to decrease the risk of mortality in all patients, but they are suspected to increase the risk of diabetes in normoglycemic patients. At the center of the controversy are pre-diabetic patients. These patients are at particularly high risk of progression to overt diabetes, yet statins appear to have no effect on their progression.*

The previous case study illustrates that the pre-diabetic patient population is particularly heterogeneous. Hypothetically, such heterogeneity would lead to differing responses to statins. Using the association rule mining mechanism described in the second case study,

Table 5-3: Risk of Diabetes in Pre-diabetic Patient Subpopulations Receiving Statins

Association Pattern	Relative Risk
Obesity, elevated blood pressure with medications	1.73*
Hyperlipidemia without medications, hypertension with medications	1.35*
Hyperlipidemia without medications, elevated blood pressure with medications	1.62*
Obesity, hyperlipidemia without medications, elevated blood pressure with medications	1.76*
Obesity, hypertension with medications, elevated blood pressure with medications	1.76*
Hyperlipidemia without medications, hypertension with medications, elevated blood pressure with medications	1.61*
Obesity, hyperlipidemia with medications	0.59
Hyperlipidemia with medications, hypertension with medications	0.59

we found subpopulations in whom statins confer an increased risk of diabetes as well as subpopulations in whom they confer a reduced risk (Table 5-3).

Thus, for example, among obese patients who have abnormally elevated blood pressure despite taking hypertension drugs, those who take statins have a 1.73 times higher risk of developing diabetes than those who do not. In contrast, among obese patients who have hyperlipidemia and take cholesterol drugs other than statins, those who take statins have lower risk than those who do not (relative risk is 0.59). The set of patterns suggests that statins significantly increase the risk of diabetes in patients who have severe hypertension (elevated blood pressure despite taking antihypertensive drugs) and possibly mild hyperlipidemia (do not take cholesterol drugs). However, statins decrease the risk of diabetes in patients with severe hyperlipidemia (who must take a combination of cholesterol drugs). These preliminary results are undergoing validation, but they highlight the clinical opportunities that data mining–based analyses can create.

CONCLUSION

The widespread use of EHRs and their integration with clinical decision support engines are on the verge of changing clinical practice. Traditionally, treatment decisions have been based on evidence gained from a single statistical model that was fit to an entire population. Building a single model is tantamount to saying that one model fits all patients, which is only possible when all patients behave similarly in terms of their outcomes and responses to interventions. Such an assumption does not hold with many diseases that are highly heterogeneous.

The Framingham diabetes index epitomizes the one-model-fits-all approach. It is based on a single additive model of approximately five easy-to-obtain risk factors to assess a patient's risk of diabetes. Because diabetes is known to be highly heterogeneous, such an approach is insufficient.

The widespread collection of data from EHRs can provide the research platform upon which data can be mined to facilitate construction of substantially more nuanced models. These models consider a wider range of potential risk factors, can identify subpopulations that behave significantly differently from the general patient population in terms of risk and response to treatment, and can consider the interactions among diseases. Finding subpopulations that have different risk factors, different risks, and different responses to a variety treatments is the key to developing a more personalized approach to clinical practice.

The increased information content of these nuanced models comes at the price of increased complexity. Paper-and-pencil application is no longer feasible. Hence, a computerized application is required. Integrating EHRs with clinical decision support (CDS) systems and implementing these nuanced models on top of the CDS systems offers the most obvious solution.

Data mining on top of the EHR and CDS systems can create a new paradigm, which can allow nuanced modeling of patient populations that encompasses a much wider variety of information. Such models may reveal new knowledge that facilitates a more personalized medicine. This is the promise of data mining and knowledge discovery from EHRs.

REFERENCES

1. Agency for Healthcare Research and Quality (AHRQ) Healthcare Cost and Utilization Project (HCUP). Clinical Classification Software. http://www.hcup-us.ahrq.gov/toolssoftware/ccs/ccs.jsp.

2. Li DC, Simon GJ, Chute CG, Pathak J. Using Association Rule Mining for Phenotype Extraction from Electronic Health Records. American Medical Informatics Association (AMIA) Clinical Research Informatics (CRI), 2013.

3. PheKB, A Knowledgebase for Discovering Phenotypes from Electronic Medical Records. http://www.phekb.org/phenotype/type-2-diabetes-mellitus.

4. Caraballo PJ, Castro MR, Cha S, Li PW, Simon GJ. Use of Association Rule Mining to Assess Diabetes Risk in Patients with Impared Fasting Glucose. Presented at American Medical Informatics Association (AMIA) Annual Symposium, 2011.

5. Simon GJ, Caraballo PJ, Therneau TM, Cha S, Castro MR, LI PW. Extending Association Rule Summarization Techniques to Assess Risk of Diabetes Mellitus. IEEE Transactions on Knowledge and Data Engineering (TKDE), 2013.

6. Schrom J, Castro MR, Caraballo PJ, Simon GJ. Quantifying the Effect of Statin Use in Pre-diabetic Phenotypes Discovered Through Association Rule Mining. American Medical Informatics Association (AMIA) Annual Symposium, 2013.

ACKNOWLEDGMENTS

The studies described in this chapter were carried out at Mayo Clinic in collaboration with Pedro J. Caraballo, MD; M. Regina Castro, MD; Peter W. Li, PhD; and Jyotishman Pathak, PhD.

CHAPTER 6

Leading and Structuring Analytics within Healthcare Organizations: The Business Intelligence Competency Center

Detlev H. Smaltz

While the level of proficiency in leveraging business intelligence is arguably nascent within most hospitals and health systems, virtually every hospital and every health system are doing something with respect to business intelligence. Invariably the quality department will have its own reporting tools and data repositories from which quality reporting is undertaken. The finance department usually has its own—typically separate—reporting tools and data repositories to support its financial reporting needs. Marketing, strategic planning, human resources, supply chain all have their own—typically siloed—approaches to analytics and reporting. "In traditional companies, departments manage analytics—number crunching functions (within those departments) select their own tools and train their own people. But that way, chaos lies."[1]

Alternatives for organizing analytics efforts within a healthcare organization along with the advantages and disadvantages of these alternatives are presented in this chapter. The concept of the Business Intelligence Competency Center (BICC) and how the BICC interacts with the rest of the healthcare organization for optimum effectiveness are discussed; as are aspects of strategic alignment and executive sponsorship that are vital to operating a successful BICC.

OPTIONS FOR ORGANIZING ANALYTIC EFFORTS WITHIN AN HCO

In the course of researching analytics for both for profit and not-for-profit companies, Davenport and colleagues[1] found five basic organizational structuring arrangements (Figure 6-1). In the centralized, consulting, and functional models, a single BI team provides most of the analytic services to the organization. The decentralized model, as its name implies, is decentralized and has no corporate oversight or coordination. With the center of excellence model, each data-consuming functional department has its

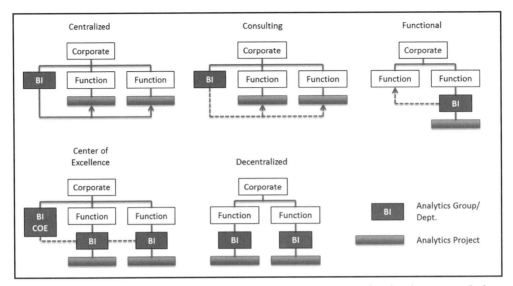

Figure 6-1: Basic organizational structuring arrangements for business analytics. Adapted from Davenport et al, 2010 – used with permission.

own analyst group, but these analysts also work with a corporate center of excellence that creates a community of practice and can double as a program office to help coordinate cross-functional projects. Each model has advantages and disadvantages (Table 6-1).

Davenport and colleagues[1] suggest that "the ideal model ensures that your scarce and valuable analysts (1) are tasked with the most important analytical projects, (2) bring an enterprise perspective to bear, and (3) have ample opportunities for development and job satisfaction. We think the centralized and center of excellence models...offer the greatest potential benefit for organizations ready to take an enterprise approach to analytics." Of note, this group's work ranges across many industries.

The healthcare industry appears to be particularly immature with respect to managing data as a strategic asset, and the predominant organizational structure is the decentralized model. Managers in health systems that believe their level of data mastery is weak should consider whether a center of excellence approach should be a first step or whether a more centralized model may need to be established initially to force change upon autonomous business units that may balk at some of the changes dictated by enterprise data management and governance. Eventually, the health system can evolve to the center of excellence model.

Gartner, an information technology (IT) industry research group, has advocated a BICC for organizations that want to develop more robust enterprise analytics capabilities.[2,3] A BICC "is a cross-functional organizational team that has defined tasks, roles, responsibilities and processes for supporting and promoting the effective use of business intelligence (BI) across an organization."[4] Other names have been used for such an organizational unit, including BI Center of Excellence, Enterprise Analytics Department, Clinical and Business Intelligence Competency Center, and Analytics Competency Center.

Table 6-1: Advantages and Disadvantages of BI Organizational Structuring Alternatives

BI Organizational Structuring Alternatives	Potential Advantages	Potential Disadvantages or Challenges
Centralized All analyst groups report to one corporate executive as a shared service	• Easier to deploy analysts on strategic projects • Easier to align priorities with overall organizational goals • Leverages business metadata standardization and economies of learning	• Can be seen as an "ivory tower" group • May be perceived as a bottleneck if governance activities are not transparent and fair
Consulting Same as centralized but not a shared service; departments "hire" analysts for projects via a "pay-to-play" methodology	• More market driven; prioritization is simplified because only projects for which departments are willing to pay are undertaken • Leverages business metadata standardization and economies of learning	• Falters under weak enterprise focus or project selection criteria and/or poor executive leadership • Functional division may attempt to build its own services if costs are high or attention is lacking
Functional A single analyst group resides in a primary data consumer's department/business unit	• Negates need for a new central department • Offers a lower-cost entry point to assess the analytics readiness of a company	• May be viewed as being too parochial to its own functional department or business unit • May lack functional analytics expertise needed by other departments
Center of Excellence Community of practice program office approach, with analyst groups decentralized but working with central corporate "program office"	• Provides autonomy of prioritization of BI projects to each decentralized analyst group • Leverages shared knowledge and experience • Leverages business metadata standardization and economies of learning • Easier to deploy analysts on strategic projects	• Can falter under weak enterprise focus or project selection criteria, particularly in the absence of a formal program office or governance prioritization approach • Can be viewed as a bottleneck if availability of resources is inadequate
Decentralized Analyst groups are associated with their respective functional departments, with little or no corporate oversight	• Provides autonomy of prioritization of BI projects to each decentralized analyst group	• Difficult to accomplish cross-functional BI projects • Difficult to set enterprise priorities • Often creates added costs due to replication of services • Data standardization may suffer

Regardless of the label given to the team designated to support enterprise analytics, Dresner and associates[2] originally suggested the following five primary functions of a BICC, which remain viable today:

- Guide users in self-service to meet their BI needs, primarily by training them how to use the data as well as how to use BI tools as a mechanism to access the data and manipulate it, which allows the BICC to have some leverage instead of having to create every report or query itself

- Perform ad hoc or complex analysis in conjunction with the business units
- Oversee the analytics approach used across the enterprise to ensure consistency
- Coordinate use and reuse of business metadata (e.g., data definitions, source of data) and business rules associated with the data
- Set standards for BI tools that are used and supported throughout the organization

In this chapter, we use the term "BICC" to refer to the team that an HCO designates to provide these functions to the entire enterprise. As noted previously, the BICC can have many different forms (e.g., centralized, consulting, functional, or center of excellence models), all of which have varying degrees of an enterprise focus.

STAFFING THE BICC

By definition, the BICC is charged with supporting and promoting the effective use of BI across an organization. Accordingly, the individuals that an organization assigns to the BICC should possess, at a minimum, representative subject matter expertise that spans the key functional data consumers of the HCO. The HCO can take a number of approaches to assure that the BICC has appropriate representative subject matter experts (SMEs), but primarily staffing involves new hires and/or leveraging external consultants or staffing from existing resources within the HCO who are reassigned to the BICC (Figure 6-2).

Among the common big data consumers in most health systems are the quality assurance and finance departments, which could provide SMEs. Other functional expertise can come from some of the other typical data consumer departments, such as strategy, operations, nursing, human resources, and ambulatory practice management. Of course, there are myriad hybrid variations of these two basic models. As with orga-

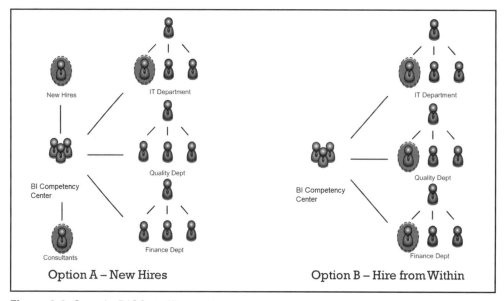

Figure 6-2: Sample BICC staffing options.

Table 6-2: Advantages and Disadvantages of Staffing Options

Staffing Option	Potential Advantages	Potential Disadvantages or Challenges
Option A Primarily new hires and external consultants	• Functional/departmental resources and productivity are not affected • Jump-starts the program with external expertise • Limited disruption to workers in their existing roles and responsibilites	• New hires and/or consultants do not know the organization and will have a longer learning curve • Functional departments/business units may not trust the efforts of new hires • Requires more "net new" resources
Option B Primarily reassigned resources from within	• BICC has organizational knowledge on day 1 • Departments that seeded the BICC with their own resources tend to trust the efforts of the BICC (instant credibility) • Requires less "net new" resources	• Functional departments may not want to let their best report writers and analysts be reassigned to an enterprise BICC that they do not directly control • Functional departments may seek to fill in the resources that were reassigned to the BICC

nizational structuring alternatives, the two basic staffing models have advantages and disadvantages (Table 6-2).

Certain organizational characteristics of an HCO can drive the decision about which of the two basic staffing options is most appropriate:

- **Full-time equivalency (FTE) growth policy.** Organizations that wish to limit their permanent FTE headcount (i.e., fully burdened salary dollars) may favor leveraging consultants at least at the outset (Option A) or reassigning resources from within (Option B).
- **Historical level of trust and cooperation between business units.** In low-trust organizations, leaders within specific functional business units may not want to see their departmental analytic resources reassigned to a corporate BICC (Option B).
- **Level of analytic expertise within the HCO.** Organizations with little reporting writing/analytic skills at their disposal may prefer leveraging new hires and/or consultants (Option A).
- **Level of leadership commitment to an enterprise approach to analytics.** Organizations without demonstrable C-level (e.g., chief executive officer, chief operating officer, chief financial officer) awareness and commitment to fostering an enterprise approach to analytics may find it difficult to reassign resources from functional departments into the BICC (Option B).

KEY BICC ROLES AND EXPERTISE

The most important role within the BICC is invariably the leader. Depending on which structuring approaches the HCO chooses, the leadership level for the BICC can range from a vice president for centralized or consulting models to a manager in a functional model. Regardless of title, the individual recruited to fill the position must have a broad understanding of the business of healthcare (ideally, both clinical and financial) and a background in data analysis or informatics. The individual also should have solid "people skills" to facilitate the cross-functional coordination that is necessary to complete BI projects successfully. Because the healthcare industry is relatively immature at managing data as a strategic asset, few healthcare BI directors or people with this type of experience are available on the open job market. Following are some potential backgrounds and experience that an HCO can look to when recruiting for this vital role:

- Nursing/clinical/medical informaticists: Individuals who typically have a grounding in report writing and analytics for the clinical/medical domain, particularly if they also have some understanding of the financial domain
- Biostatisticians: Individuals who are adept at analytics in the medical domain, particularly as BI moves from descriptive to more prospective/predictive analytics
- Leaders/managers of particular functional department analysts (e.g., financial reporting or quality analytics): These individuals must be open to learning the nuances of data and business rules associated with the other functional areas
- Vice presidents/directors/managers of analytics from the payor industry: Although these individuals may need to learn some of the nuances of provider data and business rules, they already have a grounding in analytics and a significant understanding of healthcare terminology and concepts

There is no lack of BICC leadership expertise in other industries, but understanding the context of the healthcare provider environment cannot be understated. One suggested approach is dyad leadership.[5,6] In the case of the BICC, a dyad leadership approach could partner a seasoned analytics leader who does not have the requisite healthcare background with an influential functional leader from within the HCO. The BICC led by such a dyad can:

- Overcome learning curve challenges and provide the HCO with a much larger pool of candidates for BICC leaders (e.g., the BI leader of the dyad can come from a variety of different industries)
- More easily navigate the political environment of the HCO by ensuring that the functional leader of the dyad is a well-respected, influential member of the organization
- Eventually create new functional leaders to develop deeper analytics expertise and understanding

If a BI leader with a background in healthcare is available, traditional organizational structuring models may suffice, but the dyad model of leadership should be considered if an HCO is unable to attract such a candidate.

Additional roles and expertise within the BICC should be considered as the HCO continues to expand its BI/analytics capabilities (Table 6-3).

Of course, the BICC relies heavily on the IT organization to maintain the BI tools and infrastructure of the organization (e.g., maintaining the servers that run the enterprise data warehouse [EDW]). The types of roles and numbers of personnel for a BICC vary from organization to organization. Generally, growth of the BICC should be driven by business needs. Figure 6-3 illustrates a sample timeline for staffing a BICC at a 700-bed health system with 11,000 FTEs. Ideally, an organization would start with at least one of each of the key roles, but resource constraints may dictate a smaller initial footprint for the BICC. In such cases, a BICC leader, data integrator (ETL developer/

Table 6-3: Typical Roles Within a BICC

Role	Description
Vice president/director/manager of the BICC	• Typically reports to C-level executive or the executive with responsibility for enterprise-wide business performance management/continuous process improvement/Six Sigma/Lean • Leads efforts to deliver BI infrastructure and capabilities in support of organizational performance improvement efforts and strategic initiatives; leads an enterprise BI competency center (enterprise department that is responsible for BI strategy, projects, and processes as well as training of end users on BI and ongoing BI benefits realization efforts) • Owns the enterprise data warehouse (EDW) project for organizations that have EDWs, including ensuring that sponsorship and funding are in place • Articulates the business problems that will be addressed by the BICC/EDW. • Understands BI technology and how it can be applied to solving business problems. • Tracks return on investment (ROI)/benefits achieved via various BI projects • Is the primary service provider of BI to all executives, managers, functional champions, stakeholders, and end users
Enterprise data architect	• Typically reports to BICC leader • Responsible for managing the HCO's overall data architecture, standardization, and dictionary as well as metadata associated with enterprise data (e.g., in maintaining an EDW) • Understands both hardware platforms and all software products used to support BI projects • Understands relational databases, physical/logical data models, middleware, metadata, and end-user tools • Works closely with business analysts to define data incorporated into logical data model
Data integrator (extraction, transformation & load [ETL] developer or data parser)	• Typically reports to enterprise data architect • Writes ETL scripts and parser scripts (e.g., HL7 Parsing). • Uses graphical user interface–based ETL tools • Focuses on strategic data integration issues, such as data quality/stewardship, real-time/event-based data integration, and crafting a service-oriented vision for data integration
Database administrator	• Creates, tunes, and otherwise maintains the database(s) associated with key data repositories used by the BICC (e.g., data marts or an EDW) • Reports to project manager for task management • Offers in-depth knowledge of database technology • Understands physical data models • Brings expertise in data structure (including parallel data structure) • Works closely with enterprise data architect

continued on next page

Table 6-3: *(Continued)*

Role	Description
Project manager	• Reports to the BICC leader • Understands EDW and BI project management methodology • Manages the project plan for completeness and timeliness • Manages the resource plan, ensuring that correct individuals are working toward project completion • Reports on project status • Interfaces with both EDW project team and functional stakeholders
Business analyst/data analyst	• Provides specific functional business unit expertise to serve as point of contact between the BICC and business users of the BICC's resources (such as the EDW) • Trains end users on how to navigate BICC tools and resources such as the EDW to find information • Runs reports and performs analysis • Works closely with business managers to identify requirements
BI developer	• Works closely with business analysts/data analysts to develop and publish enterprise reports, dashboards, and scorecards
Data scientist	• Has training in statistics or biostatistics • Performs data mining to detect and identify patterns in the data to inform management decision making • Leverages published predictive models or creates new predictive models and algorithms to inform management decision making

parser), enterprise data architect, and BI developer or report writer may suffice if the BICC can leverage existing database administrator and project management personnel from the IT organization.

Additionally, BI developers can serve as business/data analysts working with end users to develop initial requirements. As the need for increased BICC output grows, the addition of further resources is dictated by business needs and funded accordingly.

Typically, a data scientist is warranted once the HCO has a need to interrogate large data sets, such as those found in well-populated EDWs. Data scientists are typically trained in statistical analyses and can participate in building predictive models to help inform decision making aimed at positioning for future performance improvements.

It is important to note that there is no "one-size-fits-all" approach to staffing a BICC. The sample in Figure 6-3 is a minimal starting contingent of 4 FTEs and an approximate end state of 11 to 19 FTEs, depending on business needs of the particular HCO.

EXECUTIVE COMMITMENT AND LEADERSHIP

Effective leadership is an imperative to success in any endeavor, including analytics. Pragmatic approaches can engage leadership toward advancing an HCO's analytics capability. Two primary tactics are to:
- Create tight strategic alignment between BI projects and the HCO's goals
- Ensure that each BI initiative always has a named, engaged executive sponsor/owner

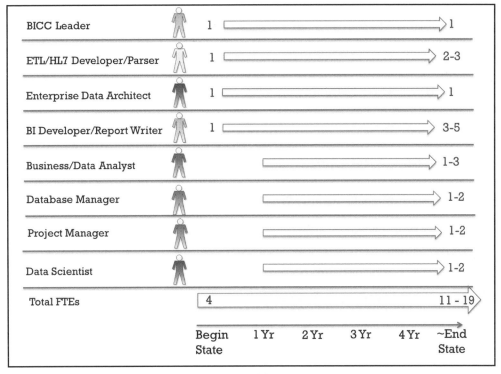

Figure 6-3: Sample timeline for staffing a BICC.

Strategic Alignment

BI initiatives tend to be more successful, enjoy greater executive visibility/sponsorship, and achieve better outcomes when they are tightly aligned with overall organizational strategic objectives. This can be accomplished by systematically and deliberately mapping the HCO's current strategic goals and objectives to BI opportunities and using the resulting document as a guiding framework for BI governance and prioritization decisions. Table 6-4 offers an example of such a strategic BI alignment, using some common themes that are representative of the overarching strategies of many contemporary health systems. Key passages within the descriptions of specific strategic objectives are highly suggestive of needs for data reporting/analytics. Articulating potential BI opportunities that could help the HCO achieve those objectives can guide enterprise BI project prioritization decisions.

Demands for new reporting and analytics invariably will increase. Organizations that have proactively vetted and achieved buy-in that priority should generally be given to those BI initiatives that help advance the HCO's overall strategic goals and objectives will find a strategic BI alignment document to be an excellent filter through which new BI requests can be weighed against other requests.

BICC Project Sponsorship

Figure 6-4 provides a graphic representation of how the BI governance activities, the BICC, and individual projects are conducted in best practice organizations. HCO BI governance has processes within its committee work to vet and select BI projects. Such

Table 6-4: Sample Strategic BI Alignment Document

Strategic Focus	Key Strategic Goal Options and Potential BI Opportunities
Become a valued partner to:	• Physicians: Strive to provide the **best possible practice experience** for all community physicians, regardless of their affiliation. **BI Alignment Opportunity: Key performance indicators (KPIs) for physician satisfaction** • Insurers: Strive to become the preferred accountable care partner for health insurers in the region by **delivering superior value through lowering the overall cost of care while maintaining top quartile quality of care, as measured by a defined set of outcomes metrics.** **BI Alignment Opportunity: KPIs by diagnosis-related group (DRG) for cost of care; KPIs by DRG for quality of care** • Employers: Strive to become the health system provider of choice for both employers and their employees based on the **ability to deliver cost-effective care with high levels of patient satisfaction.** **BI Alignment Opportunity: KPIs for employer and patient satisfaction; value-based purchasing metrics**
Develop clinical signature program	Investments in these programs are expected to deliver achievements that will advance the health system toward preeminence in: • Heart (cardiology and cardiovascular surgery; increase operating room time and resources) • Cancer (expand cancer center to cover all cancer types) • Neurosurgery (increase operating room time and resources) • Transplant (expand transplant center to include abdominal solid organ transplant and related gastroenterology, renal, and vascular programs) **BI Alignment Opportunity: Automated means to measure baseline/"before" signature program performance with "after" investment performance; KPIs to measure operating room time by signature program, number of cases, and outcomes (e.g., readmissions)**
Deliver greater value	• Maximize value for populations of patients with chronic conditions and increase disease prevention. **BI Alignment Opportunity: Value-based purchasing metrics; develop predictive analytics to better care for patients with chronic conditions and prevent admissions** • Maximize value through aggressive targeting of the lowest price point and lowest cost in the region for a hospital-based provider with top quartile quality. **BI Alignment Opportunity: Correlate quality with cost data to demonstrate this maxim**
Foster growth	• Grow geographically by natural expansion of existing service areas. **BI Alignment Opportunity: Geo-code data; ability to display data geographically** • Grow geographically by jumps in geography. **BI Alignment Opportunity: Geo-code data; ability to display data geographically** • Grow new services for new/different patients. **BI Alignment Opportunity: External data sources to find new/different patients**
Create accountability across the continuum of care	• Improve the health of the community that the health system serves through the creation of a healthcare alliance with providers in the service area that are patient focused. Break down traditional barriers and **reduce duplication and waste.** **BI Alignment Opportunity: Population health analytics; Accountable Care Organization-like analytics (leveraging interorganizational data sets from other/partner organizations to better understand opportunities to reduce duplication and waste)**

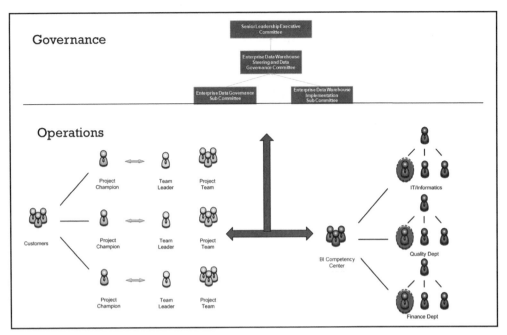

Figure 6-4: BICC project prioritization, coordination, and execution.

projects are handed to the BICC leader/dyad for execution. The BICC leader forms individual project teams composed of a business unit champion/sponsor, a team leader drawn from the BICC (typically a project manager), and other individuals (e.g., a BI developer) from the BICC as well as SMEs from key stakeholder departments or business units. For example, a new BI project to develop a clinical quality dashboard with 40 different KPIs may draw relevant SMEs from the quality department (for expertise on the Centers for Medicare & Medicaid's core measures), the emergency department (for expertise on the KPI "aspirin upon arrival," a typical quality measure relating to heart attack patients who present at the emergency department), and perhaps a nursing unit (for expertise related to KPIs related to patient safety such as patient falls). This project team is assembled and meets periodically throughout the life of the project until completion, at which time the project team is disbanded.

Contemporary HCOs suffer from a high demand for new projects and a limited supply of resources to execute them. Without an engaged, committed project champion, BICC projects can quickly languish. By aligning projects to overall strategic objectives and selecting a project champion who is committed to completion of the project, HCOs are much better positioned to achieve value from the BICC projects they undertake.

SUMMARY

As HCOs work toward handling the growing amount of data they generate and that is becoming available to the public, the need for careful and functional organization of BI is increasing. One approach that should be considered is the establishment of a BICC. A number of structuring arrangements and staffing approaches can be used to develop a BICC. Regardless of the approach used, BICC projects should be aligned with strategic organizational objectives to achieve success. Furthermore, BICC projects must be sponsored by engaged and committed functional/business unit leaders to increase the probability of gaining value from investments in the BICC.

REFERENCES

1. Davenport T, Harris J. *Competing on Analytics: The New Science of Winning*. Boston: Harvard Business School Press; 2007.

2. Dresner HJ, Buytendijk F, Linden A, et al: *The Business Intelligence Competency Center: An Essential Business Strategy*. Stamford, CT: Gartner, Inc.; 2002.

3. Strange K, Hostmann B. *BI Competency Center is Core to BI Success*. Stamford, CT: Gartner; 2003. https://www.gartner.com/doc/400976. Accessed December 2013.

4. Business intelligence competency center. *Wikipedia*. 2013. http://en.wikipedia.org/wiki/Business_Intelligence_Competency_Center. Accessed December 2013.

5. Baldwin KS, Dimunation N, Alexander J. Health care leadership and the dyad model. *Physician Exec*. 2011;37:66-70.

6. Texas health resources advances leadership, governance structures to align clinical, operational activities [press release]. Arlington, TX: Texas Health Resources; March 7, 2012. http://www.texashealth.org/mobile.cfm?id=4769&action=detail&ref=1298. Accessed December 2013.

CHAPTER 7

Data Governance: Protecting the Gold

Kim Ott and Raymond A. Gensinger, Jr.

In *The Data Asset: How Smart Companies Govern Their Data for Business Success*, Tony Fisher said that "the pressures on organizations today are ever-increasing: pressures to comply with regulatory and industry standards... pressures to compete in an uncertain and constantly changing economy."[1] This statement is especially true today in the healthcare industry. Changing reimbursement models, ever-increasing regulations, and consumer quality demands are all driving the expectation of dramatic changes in healthcare delivery. Successful organizations can use data to survive during this time of rapid change.

Many industries have understood the value of their data as strategic corporate assets, but healthcare organizations (HCOs) have been slow to recognize the power of the data they hold. In the United States, the Affordable Care Act (ACA) (also called healthcare reform), signed in March 2010, along with the Centers for Medicare & Medicaid Services (CMS) Meaningful Use program have created incentives for healthcare providers to implement electronic health records (EHRs) that can capture a wide spectrum of clinical data. Access to data for analyzing and reporting performance, designing new delivery systems, and even predicting health trends has become a requirement for the survival of HCOs. Such data are as valuable as gold and need to be carefully managed through data governance to ensure their value is both maximized and harvested. Following is a description of data governance and suggestions on how to implement an effective data governance structure.

WHAT IS DATA GOVERNANCE?

Generally, the term "data governance" describes the people, policies, and processes established by a business to make strategic enterprise decisions about one or more of the following data management areas:

Risk mitigation safeguards critical data from inappropriate disclosure. Providing optimal healthcare and appropriate patient identification requires the collection of sensitive data that include patient names, health information, Social Security numbers, insurance information, and credit card numbers. These data are routinely captured and stored electronically. Although such data enable the efficient business of healthcare, if left unprotected, they can become a major risk for the business.

Any Internet search for "theft of medical records" reveals innumerable stories about the loss or theft of medical information. Such loss occurs when laptops are stolen, unsecured emails are sent, cyber criminals hack into servers, new mobile devices freely access medical information, data are faxed to the wrong numbers, and even printed information is inappropriately left behind or mishandled. Patients worry about disclosure of their medical conditions and are concerned about identity theft. Additionally, the Privacy and Security Rules within the Healthcare Insurance Portability and Accountability Act (HIPAA) describe how sensitive data must be handled and spells out both the civil and criminal penalties for violations. A public breach of information can result in catastrophic damage to the reputation of an HCO as well as significant financial penalities.

Authorization of use addresses the responsibilities of knowing who has access to the data and for what purpose. It is one of the first components that must be addressed when working on a risk mitigation plan. Implementation of electronic applications that streamline healthcare delivery requires identification of users within the applications for appropriate authorization of activity. Usually these applications have role-based authorization schemes that work well in simple organizations, but most HCOs are complex organisms in which users often perform many functions or serve in multiple simultaneous roles. When simple roles will not accommodate the needs, the roles eventually become more generalized, allowing users to access more data than is typically necessary to complete his or her job. Tightly managing application roles and authorization through policies, controls, and resources can help to ensure that users only have access to the data they need to do their jobs.

Each application is typically tied to a database that can be accessed directly from within the application or by using database commands such as structured query language (SQL). This type of access must be limited to a very few technicians and other appropriate users to avoid the risk of data "escaping" from the organization either intentionally or accidentally.

Many HCOs have invested in some form of electronic data warehouse (EDW). Data from individual application databases are moved into the EDW for reporting or analytic purposes. Tightly controlling and monitoring who can access this vast amount of data is imperative for appropriate safeguarding of the data.

Knowing what data are leaving the HCO and how they leave is an important aspect of controlling use. The data might be sent via a simple file transfer protocol (FTP) to a research affiliate, transmitted in real-time to a healthcare data exchange, forwarded in batches to billing intermediaries, or sent one time for a special consulting engagement. Knowing where, how, and how often data are being sent and ensuring that the recipient safeguards the data are part of good data management practices.

Quality assurance (QA) ensures clean and trusted data that enables actionable decision making for all. QA efforts address data accuracy, completeness, and uniformity. Efforts to achieve QA are probably the most common reasons for an organization to undertake data governance.

QA processes work hand-in-hand with data stewards to ensure that data are captured in recognizable, consistent formats across the organization or that inconsistently captured data are reformatted into a consistent pattern. A classic example of "dirty" data is the myriad ways that telephone numbers can be captured. Each of the following represents the same telephone number: 612-555-1234 or 6125551234 or (612)555-1234 or 555-1234. Inconsistency in the recording of such data can have results equivalent to completely erroneous recording. Any computer-aided analysis application may view each entry as a different number. To combat the problem, data cleansing techniques are used to transform each telephone number into a uniform data format.

Sometimes QA work focuses on education that ensures accuracy in how the data are captured initially. For decades, clinicians were taught that rounding blood pressure readings to the nearest 5 mm Hg was sufficient, so that a systolic reading of 138 or 139 was rounded to 140. Today's more sophisticated decision support algorithms and quality reporting programs require far more accurate blood pressure readings. In a marketplace where providers are paid for outcomes, the recording of a blood pressure at 140 rather than 138 can mean the difference between unsatisfactory and appropriate management of a patient who has hypertension.

QA processes can also detect and help correct incomplete data. Missing data diminish the ability to provide actionable information. Educating users who capture the data about the data's downstream value can increase data completeness, and sometimes data cleansing rules can fill in missing data. For example, if the state field on a form is blank but the zip code is entered, an automated data cleansing rule could look up and fill in the missing state information.

Data lifecycle management oversees how data enter and are retained by the organization as well as how they are purged or archived. Defining how data are managed for the organization has financial risks and benefits. Typically, the data governance body implements a set of policies that govern how data are used by the organization. The policies become the rules used by information technology (IT) departments to manage the data effectively.

Legal risk is migated by retaining the right amount of data, keeping only that which is required and destroying the rest. Knowing the right amount of data to keep can be challenging. It is governed by many rules created by CMS and legal precedence. The compliance and health information management (HIM) departments can provide advice. For example, they should know the specific pediatric healthcare data retention policies that require data to be maintained for a longer period of time than needed for adult data.

Even as the cost of storage continues to decrease, the amount of data that organizations must manage is growing even faster. Storage is a very large IT expense. Using lifecycle management policies, the IT department can separate data into tiers, typically layered newest data to oldest. Once tiers are established, the IT department can manage storage costs by migrating data from fast (most expensive) storage to slower (less expensive) storage and ultimately free up storage space by purging or archiving to alternate media.

Prioritizing investments is the process of ranking and funding appropriate data initiatives for the company. There are always more demands than resources to complete the work. The data governance body can help to set priorities. Transparency about the magnitude of the work, what methods are used to prioritize the work, and what work remains in the backlog can help the HCO understand and support funded efforts.

Data literacy is designed to mature the organization's ability to provide meaningful data for effective decision making.[2] At its simplest, developing a program of data literacy includes education and assessment about how to understand and evaluate raw data, then interpret graphs and charts to answer complex business and clinical questions. This effort helps people find, manipulate, interpret, and scrutinize data. It is a unifying effort for decision makers across the organization. All management staff should be comfortable reading and interpreting a control chart, should understand the implications of precise versus rounded recording of data, and should be able to ask provocative questions about the data represented.

Standardization involves use of industry standard terminologies (e.g., LOINC, CPT, ICD, SNOMEDCT). Standards enable an organization to speak a common language without needing to define the language. The more often a standard is used when capturing data, the more often the data can be repurposed without ambiguity, both within the organization and when sharing data outside the organization. The Healthcare Information Technology Standards Panel (HITSP) works to establish standards for sharing clinical and business data between HCOs. Internally, an organization may want to implement a master data management (MDM) service to ensure standard master files across the organziation. MDM is often used to manage provider identifiers, patient identifiers, location codes, and other fundamental data.

Managing complexity is required to reduce ambiguity about the meaning of data by fostering common understanding and eliminating redundant data sources. Driving out complexity can unveil difficult choices. Which is the source of truth: data stored in the laboratory system or those same data within the patient's EHR? Is the definition of an admission the same at all hospitals within the system? Does one organization include patients who are being observed in their admissions count while others do not? Why is the organization using different applications to support the same business process? Does every location use the same alogrithm to attribute patients to providers?

Artifacts of work that reduce ambiguity include an enterprise data glossary, definitive sources of truth, and enterprise-level diagrams describing applications and their business process intersections. By reducing the number of applications that capture the same data, an organization saves money in IT expenses for licenses and infrastructure and reduces expenses indirectly by eliminating time spent debating optimal data sources.

WHAT IS INVOLVED IN ESTABLISHING DATA GOVERNANCE?

Data governance implementations vary widely in scope, areas of focus, and forms. Only mature organizations can take on all aspects of data governance. Effective healthcare analytics programs rely on clean, trusted data, so many HCOs begin their data governance programs by focusing on data quality. Additionally, typical data governance groups create and ensure compliance with policies, guidelines, and business rules that determine how data are used by the organization. Once those processes are in place and functioning smoothly, expanding the scope of data governance is much simpler than trying to start with all aspects at once. The following questions can help an HCO determine its initial focus area.

Is your organization focusing on making better decisions or is it ready to explore business intelligence and analytics?

Good decisions require good data. The initial focus should be on data quality, data controls, and data literacy. Having data governance begin with the fundamentals of trusted data can improve organizational understanding of the data and instill greater confidence in the data and subsequent decision making on which it is based.

Is your organization moving from a segregated or siloed view to an enterprise view of the world?

An enterprise view requires everyone in the HCO to understand the data and their implications regardless of where they are being viewed within the organization. The first step is to focus on standard definitions of processes that include master data identification. Common understanding of the data and consistent calculations and representations can unify the organization by eliminating unnecessary variation that prevents understanding from one part of the business to another.

Is your organization concerned that sensitive or private data are at risk of inappropriate disclosure?

Digital data are easily transported and misplaced. Such actions may be intentional, but the occurrence is far more likely to be incidental. Risks can be mitigated in this situation by focusing on understanding where that data are and establishing policies on how the data are used and managed. Such policies should define where data should be stored, who has access and under what circumstances, and the mechanisms or expectations required to allow data transport. This can keep sensitive business data from slipping into inappropriate hands or lost patient information from becoming front-page news.

Is your organization struggling with knowing what data-related activity to tackle first?

The hunger of an organization for knowledge is manifested through requests for reports and reporting tools. Similar to other technology services, not every request can be delivered within the desired time frame. Establishing a data governance prioritization committee with defined guiding principles can align the organization's knowledge efforts with the overall corporate strategy.

Does your organization have myriad applications with overlapping functionality and, therefore, do you need to manage complexity?

Organizational size, complexity, and consolidation result in duplication of applications and data collection methodologies. Consolidation adds value and clarity, but reconciliation to a standard approach can be taxing. A data governance committee can be leveraged to make the difficult choices on which applications (and data) become the corporate standard or source of truth. This exercise not only discloses the level of duplication but also identifies risks of variation that may not have been previously known.

Is your organization working to reduce costs?

Application duplication, data duplication (not to mention primary applications and databases that may be duplicated for business continuity purposes), and the repetitive manual processing that occurs across those applications add to organizational overhead. By focusing data governance efforts on the reduction of duplicate data sources, the HCO can reduce complexity and unnecessary redundancy while providing clarity and ultimately reducing operational and maintenance costs.

WHAT ROLES AND RESPONSIBILITES ARE NEEDED FOR DATA GOVERNANCE?

Data governance is a business leadership challenge that requires collaboration at many levels of the organization and across diverse business stakeholders. Data governance looks beyond organizational boundaries to determine who is accountable for what areas of the business and for setting policies and standards for data use. Successful organizations place accountability for data governance at the highest levels. Corporate data assets are as valuable as gold, and protecting and using those assets needs the same level of scrutiny as is exercised for other corporate assets. Executive-level visibility and accountability for data goverance are crucial to launching an effective data governance program.

The roles needed for data governance vary, based on the organization, but a typical structure includes several key roles (Figure 7-1).

The data governance committee is an executive steering committee, sponsored by a C-level executive who is an active participant and committed to improvement. The committee is composed of executive leadership, key data stakeholders, and IT leadership. Its work is facilitated by a progam manager, who typically has data management responsibilities. If there are overlapping business interests, the committee provides oversight to create clarity and balance. It endorses policies and rules and champions the need for data-driven decision making. The data governance committee understands that advanced analytics is key to the future success of HCOs and continually reinforces the importance of treating the corporate data like gold. There is no substitute for strong leadership.

The program manager has the primary responsibility of being an unbiased facilitator who ensures that the work of data governance continues. As the C-level executive chairs the committee, the program manager is the key supporting staff member. Together they ensure the smooth functioning of the data governance program by managing agendas and schedules; communicating to stakeholders; tracking progress, issues, and decisions; escalating issues for resolution; and coordinating data stewards.

Data stakeholders are line-of-business managers from all aspects of the business who care about the data. They typically oversee areas that produce data, and they use data from multiple lines of business to make decisions. These users of data are key participants in the Data Governance Committee, approving data policies and evangelizing good data practices.

Data stewards are numerous in a mature data governance structure and often work in front-line positions for the business. The best data stewards are well-respected subject matter experts for their area. They must be strong communicators and have a good

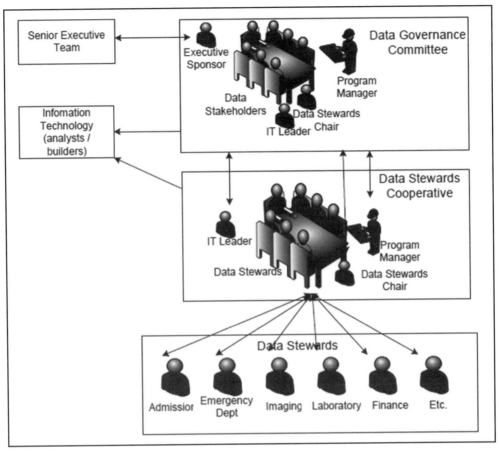

Figure 7-1: Example of data governance structure with key roles.

understanding of how their domain of data affects business processes and decisions. They should be asked to improve their data's quality, completeness, timeliness, reliability, and correctness; provide definitions for the data; and proactively prevent issues with data. Their expertise is required to ensure that the organization clearly understands the data and, through educational efforts, avoids false interpretations of the data. Typically, data stewards report to a data stakeholder, but they may also have a dotted-line relationship to the executive sponsor of data governance. Additionally, data stewardship accountabilities are often added to both data steward and data stakeholder job descriptions.

The data steward cooperative is a forum where data stewards, who work independently across many lines of business, can form a community of practice. In the data steward cooperative meetings, data stewards can share experiences, determine tools to use and consistent methods of using them, strategize on training techniques, draft data governance policies and recommendations for endorsement by the data governance committee, and learn from each other to mature the practices of data stewardship. An elected data stewards chairperson typically provides a communication conduit between the data stewards and the data governance committee. The progam manager can help with the logistics of the meeting, and an IT leader should attend to ensure that concepts are communicated back to the IT department.

The IT leader can ensure that policies and rules related to data governance can be executed and supported by the IT department. IT leadership must actively participate and consult about data governance processes. IT does not run or direct data governance activities, but this department often can identify potential difficulties and raise concerns to the accountable business area for consideration.

GUIDING PRINCIPLES

One of the first tasks of the governing body is to establish a framework of principles to expedite decision making and provide a sense of transparency to assist the entire HCO in understanding how and why decisions are being made. Some example principles include:

- **Organizational data are considered an enterprise asset owned by the company.** The data are not owned by any indivdual or department and will be shared within the organization and appropriately governed before being shared outside of the organization.
- **Except where explicitly restricted, the enterprise data will be accessible.** The organization is starting with the expectation that people have access to the data they need to do their job and that the organization's responsibility is to define those data that require expressed release (e.g., Social Security numbers, credit card numbers, certain diagnoses).
- **Industry standards for data will be used everywhere possible.** A set of standards will be identified and all data will be converted to those standards. In addition, any new contracts and relationships will be expected to use those same standards.
- **Debate about data's meaning will be discouraged.** Data definition and business context are documented and maintained in an accessible centralized repository accessible to all.
- **All employees must know that proper use of enterprise data is critical to the organization's success.** Training and auditing are the minimum expectations for those who have responsibility for creating and working with data to illustrate examples of the impact of proper and improper data stewardship.
- **Enterprise data must be protected.** Data will not be released outside of the organization, except with permission or defined contractual obligations.
- **As much as possible, data will be captured in one place.** Data will be captured at its source. Redundancy must be justified and reconciled.

WHAT CAN BE BOUGHT?

Data governance start-up expertise can be purchased. Consulting companies offer services that analyze the type of data governance needed for an HCO. Consultants can create plans and roadmaps, provide governance structure ideas, define processes, suggest adoption techniques, and faciliate the initial governance meetings. However, data governance is not a short-term effort; it requires ongoing organizational commitment.

In many respects, data governance represents a change to the organization's culture, and merely establishing policies and rules does not guarantee good data management practices. Only inspired organizational change agents (who are part of the governance process) can spread the message every day. Such resources cannot be bought, and they are crucial to an effective data governance program.

Also available for purchase are software data governance tools that primarily are designed to enable data quality improvements. These tools can provide:

- A business glossary to reduce confusion by providing a single central repository for capturing and sharing data definitions and the business context for the data.
- Metadata capture and maintenance that records the lineage of data, showing the source of the data and any adjustments made to it. This typically technical information about the data, when combined with a business glossary, provides a full understanding of the data element.
- Data cleansing and matching rules-based detection and correction of data anomalies.
- Data profiling and discovery to help the user understand how the data look, identify inconsistencies, and determine where data can be found.

Investing in tools can be useful, but the tools are only as good as the skilled personnel who use them. Software data governance tools can be delivered as part of a professional services program, but nothing substitutes for ongoing, committed organizational resources. A transition plan moving from a consultation service through education and training and subsequently to organizational independence should be considered.

SUMMARY

Corporate data are precious and can deliver great value when trusted, understood, and used in effective decision making. Data governance principles and practices are key to making the best use of the organization's "data gold." The value of gold that is polished with data quality techniques, protected, and shared within the organization compounds visibly. As he provided the important opening words in this chapter on data governance, we leave the final words to Tony Fisher: "Data governance is an evolutionary process. It cannot be done overnight, or by next quarter, or in time for the annual meeting. It is a process that even the most mature companies strive to reach every day. But it can be done. And you can be the force to make it happen."[1]

Data Governance Start-up Checklist

1) Identify C-level sponsor
2) Use an assessment to determine high-value focus area(s)
3) Develop guiding principles/charter(s)
4) Describe roles, responsibilities, and authorities for governance participants
   a. Governance committee
   b. Data stakeholders
   c. IT leaders
   d. Data stewards
   e. Program manager
      i. Determine logistics to connect participants
      ii. Track progress and maintain roadmap
5) Build a set of templates to enable data governance processes
   a. Evaluate marketplace tools
6) Identify subject area domains
7) Assign data stewards to subject area domains
   a. Clearly communicate accountabilities and authorities
8) Create a library of training materials
9) Craft performance measures
10) Deliver regular communication

REFERENCES

1. Fisher T. *The Data Asset: How Smart Companies Govern Their Data for Business*. Hoboken, NJ: John Wiley & Sons, Inc.; 2009.

2. Data literacy. *Wikipedia*. 2013. http://en.wikipedia.org/wiki/Data_literacy. Accessed October 2013.

BIBLIOGRAPHY

Adler S. *A Flash-light into the Dark: The Starters Guide to Data Governance*. Armonk, NY: IBM Corporation; 2007.

http://www-07.ibm.com/events/au/iod/downloads/IPS6_Data-Governance.pdf. Accessed September 2013.

Aiken P. *Making the Case for Data Governance*. Glen Allen, VA: Data Bluprint; 2012. http://www.aiim.org/documents/chapters/olddominion/Making_the_Case_for_DG.pdf. Accessed October 2013.

Chen W. *Kalido Data Governance Maturity Model*. Burlington, MA: Kalido; 2010. http://www.kalido.com/Collateral/Documents/English-US/Kalido-Data-Governance-Maturity-Model-1-5.pdf. Accessed September 2013.

Data Governance – 8 Steps to Success, Anne Marie Smith, Ph.D, 13 March, 2013. http://www.dama-phila.org/AMSmith-DataGovernance-8Steps.pdf, page last viewed 28 September, 2013.

Data Governance: The Basic Information. The Data Manager's Public Library. Orlando, FL: The Data Governance Institute. http://www.datagovernance.com/adg_data_governance_basics.html. Accessed September 2013.

Driving Value from Your Healthcare Analytics Program, Edgewater Consulting. 2010. http://blog.edgewater.com/category/enterprise-information-management-eim/page/3/. Accessed October 2013.

Faloney M. Increased focus on governance at HIMSS 2011. *Perficient*. 2011. https://blogs.perficient.com/healthcare/blog/2011/02/21/increased-focus-on-governance-at-himss-2011/. Accessed September 2013.

Guess A. Data governance checklist for educators. *Dataversity*. 2011. http://www.dataversity.net/?s=data+governance+checklist+for+educators. Accessed October 2013.

HIMSS Clinical & Business Intelligence Community of Practice, 27 June, 2013. Chicago, IL: Healthcard Information and Management Systems Society. 2013. http://himss.files.cms-plus.com/2013-06-27_%20DELTA-Powered-Analytics-Assessment_HIMSS%20CBI.pdf. Accessed September 2013.

Lawson L. What CIOs should know about data tools and vendor hype. *IT Business Edge*. 2012. C7 Ott Data-Governance final edits_RG.docxhttp://www.itbusinessedge.com/cm/community/features/interviews/blog/what-cios-should-know-about-data-tools-and-vendor-hype/?cs=50531. Accessed October 2013.

Loshin D. Guideline 1: Understand how corporate business drivers depend on information. *Embarcadero Technologies*. 2012. http://www.embarcadero.com/blog/guideline-1-understand-business-drivers/. Accessed October 2013.

Loshin D. Guideline 3: define data governance roles and responsibilities. *Embarcadero Technologies*. 2012. C7 Ott DataGovernance final edits_RG.docxhttp://www.embarcadero.com/blog/?s=guideline+3+define+data+governance. Accessed October 2013.

Seiner RS. Data governance core principles. *The Data Administration Newsletter*. 2013. http://www.tdan.com/view-articles/17087. Accessed October 2013.

Seiner RS. Data steward roles & responsibilities. *The Data Administration Newsletter*. 2005. http://www.tdan.com/view-articles/5236. Accessed September 2013.

Seiner RS. The data governance bill of "rights." *The Data Administration Newsletter*. 2013. http://www.tdan.com/view-articles/17042. Accessed October 2013.

Stiglich P. Data governance and data stewardship—keys to successful enterprise data initiatives. *Perficient*. 2012. http://blogs.perficient.com/healthcare/blog/2012/01/09/data-governance-and-data-stewardship-keys-to-successful-enterprise-data-initiatives/. Accessed September 2013.

Stiglich P. Data governance and stewardship organizations. *Perficient*. 2012. http://blogs.perficient.com/healthcare/blog/2012/06/18/data-governance-and-stewardship-organizations/. Accessed September 2013.

Stiglich P. Healthcare data modeling governance. *Perficient*. 2013. http://blogs.perficient.com/healthcare/blog/2013/05/29/healthcare-data-modeling-governance/. Accessed September 2013.

The Data Governance Maturity Model: Establishing the People, Policies and Technology That Manage Enterprise Data. Cary, NC: DataFlux Corporation, SAS Institute, Inc. http://www.sas.com/offices/NA/canada/lp/DIDQ/DataFlux.pdf. Accessed September 2013.

Thomas G. *The DGI Data Governance Framework*. Orlando, FL: The Data Governance Institute. http://www.datagovernance.com/dgi_framework.pdf. Accessed September 2013.

CHAPTER 8

The DELTA Analytics Maturity Model

James E. Gaston

In the preceding chapters, authors have laid out the case for, and the elements of, a successful analytics program within any healthcare organization (HCO). They have offered novel insights for building and using those programs, but not every organization has the fortitude, skill, or bandwidth to take on such initiatives. We offer an approach for assessing and jump-starting an analytics strategy. This is not meant to be the definitive approach; rather, it is built upon the ideas of well-respected authors and executed via the recognized and respected HIMSS Analytics organization. Readers will need to choose their own approaches, but we suggest a definitive starting point.

The backbone of the DELTA Powered™ benchmark and maturation model is the DELTA Analytics Maturity Model introduced by Davenport and Davis in their well-known book *Competing on Analytics*[1] and expanded upon in *Analytics at Work*.[2] By creating a healthcare-oriented version of a standard analytics maturity model that is well known and accepted in the industry as well as endorsed by leading organizations, HIMSS Analytics and the International Institute for Analytics (IIA) seek to further the advancement of healthcare analytics and provide guidance, benchmarking, and clarity for the future.

To benchmark healthcare readiness in analytics, HIMSS Analytics and IIA created a survey tool. With established benchmarks, survey participants can gain greater insight into how well their healthcare organizations leverage clinical and business intelligence (BI) and analytics in relation to both their own and other industries. Participants learn how they perform in the five critical success areas outlined in the DELTA model (Figure 8-1). In addition, they can discern existing opportunities for improving the impact of analytics in their organizations as well as how to mature core competencies. The healthcare-oriented DELTA Powered™ Maturation Roadmap outlined in this chapter can guide HCOs through this journey. IIA (www.HIMSSAnalytics.org/DELTA) offers additional opportunities and services for the use of and maturation of analytics within HCOs.

The DELTA Powered Analytical Assessment measures maturity by profiling analytic perceptions and importance across five foundational areas:

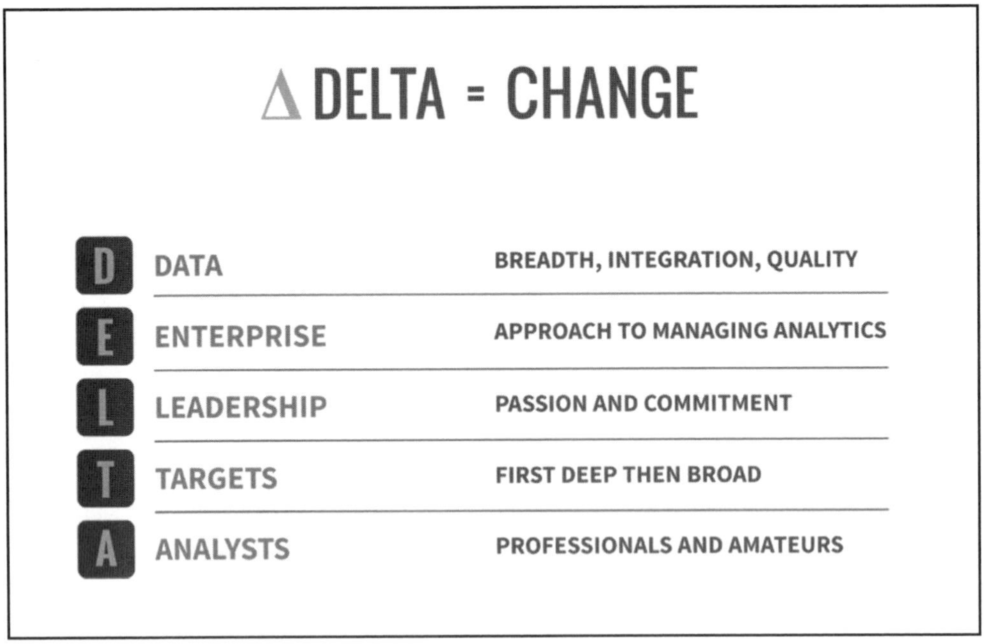

△ DELTA = CHANGE

D	DATA	BREADTH, INTEGRATION, QUALITY
E	ENTERPRISE	APPROACH TO MANAGING ANALYTICS
L	LEADERSHIP	PASSION AND COMMITMENT
T	TARGETS	FIRST DEEP THEN BROAD
A	ANALYSTS	PROFESSIONALS AND AMATEURS

Figure 8-1: Critical success areas in the DELTA model.

Data encompasses the breadth, integration, and quality of data in the organization. Good data form the prerequisite for any analytic activity, and the data must be clean, that is, accurate and consistently formatted.

Enterprise involves the approach to managing analytics in the organization. Enterprise ownership of the important data as well as analytic software and talent are critical because significant analytic initiatives, by their very nature, cross organizational boundaries and functions.

Leadership in the organization must be committed to leveraging analytics. In addition to being committed to analytics projects, leaders must have a passion for managing with data and expect the rest of the organization to do so. They must be champions of the value of being data driven in decision making and using analytics to drive strategy.

Targets must be identified for the most effective use of analytics. Analysts are a scarce resource, and applying them to strategic, high-value targets such as customer loyalty, supply chain efficiency, medical error reductions, cost reduction, and improved patient outcomes can insure that those resources are used to their highest potential. Because there are never enough analysts to address all business problems, good organizations define the problems of highest importance.

Analysts are, in many senses, the engine behind analytics. They are just as critical as the data and software. Organizations leverage analysts not only to develop and deploy models but also to bring analytics into the organization by assisting the business with identifying opportunities to apply analytics.

WHAT IS AND WHY SEEK ANALYTICS MATURITY?

"Analytics" is defined by Wikipedia as the discovery and communication of meaningful patterns in data.[3] Few industries have more data than healthcare. Years ago almost all patient and healthcare business data were manually collected and stored in individual patient charts that were secured in individual offices or hospital basements. Now healthcare is in the process of transitioning to electronic health records (EHRs) that are readily available to both physicians and patients via mobile electronic devises. EHRs allow the collection and management of data to advance the clinical and business aspects of healthcare.

The healthcare industry is undergoing a transformational change driven by federal healthcare reform, with a focus on decreasing costs and improving quality. New concepts such as "meaningful use," "accountable care," and migration from fee-for-service to quality- and patient-centered care have created a greater need to apply and refine healthcare-oriented analytics. No longer can HCOs simply focus on operational processes and efficiencies; the market is driving out activity that has no concern for costs or quality. HCOs must gain a greater understanding of what is happening within their organizations as well as with individual patients and the larger patient populations they serve. This requires a move beyond gut instinct to trending and tracking specific data that drive their business and quality of care. Thus, analytics, the discovery and communication of meaningful patterns in healthcare data, has become a critical force in healthcare reform.

Many other industries have already effectively leveraged analytics to advance their businesses. Organizations such as FedEx, Google, and Walmart, to name a very few, have applied analytics and BI to gain competitive advantages that competitors find hard to duplicate or counter. Using techniques such as advanced analytics (e.g., predictive modeling, marketing optimization, risk analysis) and BI (e.g., reporting, online analytical processing, analytics, data mining, text mining), other industries have led the way in analytics solutions, approaches, tools, and success. Leveraging "big data" (larger and even external data sets), effective and pervasive BI, mobile technology, cloud computing, and other advances in technology and data management are common in many industries other than healthcare.

Healthcare can no longer ignore the opportunities that analytics has provided to other industries. The needs for care management, quality management, and cost control have reached a nadir. Beginning on a path toward analytics maturity can give direction to HCOs, enabling meaningful transformation of their services to add value to customers and improve organizational performance. The generally slow adoption of information technology (IT) and creation of data silos highlights the substantial room for improvement in HCOs. An analytics maturity model provides a critical framework for structure, focus, and an efficient path to improvement.

HIMSS ANALYTICS MATURITY MODEL HISTORY

HIMSS Analytics has historically provided benchmarks and maturity models to assist HCOs in measuring and planning their adoption of healthcare IT. In 2004, HIMSS acquired the Dorenfest IHDS+ Database™, which was renamed the HIMSS Analytics® Database, and used it to create understanding of healthcare IT deployment across the United States and internationally. HIMSS Analytics devised the electronic medical record (EMR) Adoption Model (EMRAM) (Figure 8-2),[4] an 8-stage maturity model that tracks the IT adoption progress of HCOs and presents national and regional adoption comparisons and research.

This model was followed by the Ambulatory EMR Adoption Model[SM] (A-EMRAM),[5] seen as the next-generation tool for monitoring EMR adoption in ambulatory settings. This evaluation model creates a framework for dialogue among ambulatory facilities by providing the needed focus on vital IT systems that must be implemented to achieve higher levels of access, quality, efficiency, and safety; progress

United States EMR Adoption Model[SM]	
Stage	**Cumulative Capabilities**
Stage 7	Complete EMR; CCD transactions to share data; Data warehousing; Data continuity with ED, ambulatory, OP
Stage 6	Physician documentation (structured templates), full CDSS (variance & compliance), full R-PACS
Stage 5	Closed loop medication administration
Stage 4	CPOE, Clinical Decision Support (clinical protocols)
Stage 3	Nursing/clinical documentation (flow sheets), CDSS (error checking), PACS available outside Radiology
Stage 2	CDR, Controlled Medical Vocabulary, CDS, may have Document Imaging; HIE capable
Stage 1	Ancillaries - Lab, Rad, Pharmacy - All Installed
Stage 0	All Three Ancillaries Not Installed

Figure 8-2: EMRAM. From HIMSSAnalytics.org website.

toward meaningful use requirements; align business strategies; and compare progress against other ambulatory facilities.

Although effective implementation of IT is a good initial step, the real power comes from employing these solutions to collect data that can be used to engage the HCO in a continuous improvement cycle across both clinical and business areas. "Analytics" is defined as discovering meaningful patterns in data and effectively communicating those patterns.[3]

COLLABORATION

The IIA[6] believes that analytics is the most compelling competitive differentiator in business today. However, few organizations are confident in their ability to successfully build, fund, and prioritize a competitive analytics initiative. HCOs face additional challenges when focusing on analytics because of the industry's historically late and slow adoption of technology. Recent Affordable Care Act (ACA) and other government mandates have increased the need to implement EHRs and other technology-based solutions. Such significant changes in the environment create opportunities for the healthcare industry to mature its use of analytics, and IIA has a unique and exceptional understanding of the analytics space. This is why HIMSS Analytics decided to collaborate with IIA, an organization that has focused on understanding and refining analytic maturity across many industries, to provide insight and vision to HIMSS Analytics constituents.

IIA is the only research firm dedicated exclusively to defining the path to analytics excellence. Its faculty provides critical resources and an inspired view into how enterprises can meet both the demand and opportunities for analytic intelligence in everyday decisions. Their research-based approach offers the reliability of a world-class research library and faculty team, the benefits of a professional association, and the inspiration of a face-to-face network. IIA strives to set the highest standards of professional insights, with a rigorous commitment to quality research that generates actionable, repeatable, and transferable practices for their clients.

HIMSS Analytics, with a passion to help HCOs know "what's next", has collaborated with IIA to present a healthcare-oriented version of the DELTA Analytics Maturity Model that allows healthcare providers to assess their analytic maturity. In addition, HIMSS Analytics has created a healthcare-specific Analytics Maturity Roadmap and associated Analytics Maturity Certification Program. These three components comprise a DELTA Powered™ suite of services that HCOs can use to assess, mature, and optimize their use of clinical and business intelligence (C&BI) as well as analytics in a way that is effective, measureable, benchmarked, and strategically aligned within their organizations.

THE DELTA POWERED™ SUITE

DELTA Powered™ Analytics Assessment

The DELTA Powered Analytics Assessment represents a first step toward understanding an HCO's analytic maturity and formulating a plan for optimization. The Analytics Assessment uses a web-based survey to collect organizational importance and effective-

Table 8-1: Five Ascending Maturity Model Stages

Maturity Level	Overall DELTA Score	Requirements
Level 5: Analytical Leader	4.0 – 5.0	Survey ≥3% employee participation, case study, on-site review
Level 4: Analytically Capable	3.0 – 3.9	Survey ≥3% employee participation, case study
Level 3: Analytically Aspiring	2.0 – 2.9	Survey ≥2.5% participation
Level 2: Localized Analytics	1.0 – 1.9	Survey ≥15 participants
Level 1: Analytical Beginner	0.0 – 0.9	Survey ≥15 participants

ness data across 33 analytic competencies from analytics users, providers, and enablers. These survey data are used to create a quantitative measurement of organizational analytic maturity, with results presented in a multipart report slide deck. The results include comparisons against healthcare industry and other industry benchmarks.

The assessment delivers an industry agnostic numerical measurement of an HCO's analytical maturity across the five previously cited foundational areas of the DELTA mode and provides an overall numeric composite score representing overall analytical maturity. These numerical measurements translate into the five ascending maturity model stages (Table 8-1).

The survey is coordinated by an organization sponsor, who works with HIMSS Analytics and IIA to facilitate the survey at the HCO. The sponsor provides demographic data as well as a listing of organization users, creators, and enablers of analytics. A minimum of 15 survey participants is required, but greater accuracy in results is achieved with more participants. The participants should come from all areas of the organization, ranging from human resources and finance to administration and housekeeping, to identify the breadth and depth of analytics across the entire enterprise.

Assessment participants rank the importance of and the effectiveness with which the HCO engages in the model's 33 core competencies. The survey requires approximately 15 to 20 minutes for each participant to complete. The results can identify perception gaps between users, providers, and enablers of analytics that may be significant as well as provide insight into specific growth opportunities.

Participating HCOs receive a custom-created report derived from their assessment data that includes DELTA-overall and by-DELTA-area scoring, benchmarking, and other critical and relevant analyses. HCOs have the opportunity to acquire additional enhanced reporting; collect and divide data by specific constituency groups; and have the results presented to organizational leaders for use in establishing an organizational benchmark, analytical vision, or strategy (Figure 8-3).

DELTA Powered™ Maturity Roadmap

The DELTA Powered Maturity Roadmap provides a basic route for HCOs interested in moving their capabilities forward across the five DELTA foundational areas. By linking the DELTA Powered Analytics Assessment survey results by DELTA foundational area with the DELTA Powered Maturity Roadmap, HCOs can effectively manage specific key milestones and organizational activities to plot a course toward improved analytical

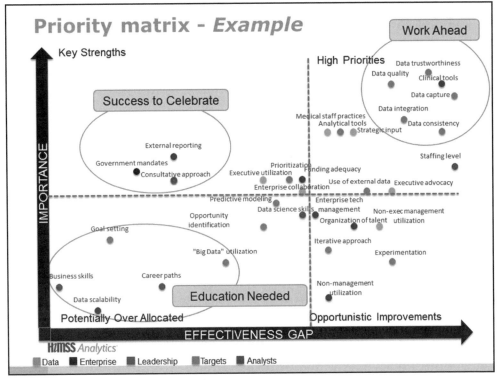

Figure 8-3: Sample matrix for HCO priorities.

capability and results. The Maturity Roadmap provides specific capabilities and competencies for each of the five core competency areas and for each of the five maturity levels from "Beginner" through "Leader" (Figure 8-4).

Each of the five levels has specific core competencies that must be developed to a mature state before moving to the next level. Some HCOs may decide that becoming a Level 5 Leader is absolutely necessary; other organizations may balance the costs and effort of analytical maturity against their resources and market demands and determine that a lower level of analytical maturity is most appropriate. Whatever level is appropriate for a particular HCO, using the Analytical Assessment and the associated Maturity Roadmap can engage the organization in a conversation about analytics and provide a framework for reaching a conclusion about the appropriate level of analytical maturity.

The most important key qualifiers for a given maturity level (Figure 8-4) represent in very brief terms some of the competencies that an HCO should be expected to demonstrate proficiently at the specific level of analytical maturity. Additional details and examples of competencies for each level are further defined later in this chapter.

More detailed information about the characteristics that provide an in-depth look at the DELTA maturity model can be found in *Analytics at Work*.[2] This well-known publication is the definitive guide to the DELTA Analytics Maturity Model. HIMSS Analytics and IIA have used this model to create a model that incorporates healthcare language, business practices, and related knowledge. Over time, HIMSS Analytics will work to refine the healthcare appeal and details of the DELTA Powered suite further.

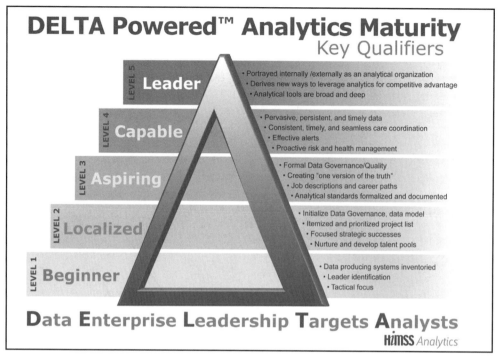

Figure 8-4: The DELTA Powered Analytics Maturity Model as adapted for healthcare. From Davenport TH, Harris J, Morison R. *Analytics at Work.*[2]

DELTA Powered™ Certification

Certification provides motivation and recognition to HCO leadership and staff for achieving progress in their efforts to become analytically mature. Certification levels and scoring align with DELTA model stages (Beginner, Localized, Aspiring, Capable, and Leader) and reflect assimilation of individual DELTA foundational area survey scores across Data, Enterprise, Leadership, Targets, and Analysts. DELTA Powered Certification for "Capable" and "Leader" HCOs (the two highest tiers) have additional case study and site visit requirements similar to Stage 6 and Stage 7 EMRAM program requirements.

DELTA POWERED™ MATURITY ROADMAP DETAILS

The symbol delta represents change, and measuring the progress of change in the five foundational areas across an organization is what the DELTA Analytics Maturity Model is designed to do. An HCO can be described in DELTA terms from a beginner to a leading state. These generic organization qualities[2] have been augmented to apply specifically to healthcare in some cases.

Stage 1: Analytical Beginner
"Not data-driven." Rely on gut feel and plan to keep doing so. The organization isn't asking analytics questions and/or lack the data to answer them.
- The HCO lacks one or several prerequisites for serious analytical work, such as data, analytical skills, or senior management interest.[1] HIMSS Analytics terms

this "Stage 1: Analytical Beginner" to put a positive perspective on where the HCO is and what can be achieved.

- The organization may have data in operational systems, but they are not accessible for ad hoc or external analytics. Tools may have been purchased and even installed, but they are limited or no staff is trained. Further, integration of analytics into decision, business, or clinical processes is neither pursued nor encouraged. Data are incomplete and isolated, difficult to acquire, and of poor quality. Analytical resources such as researchers, if present, are isolated and not encouraged.
- Analytics are haphazard or nonexistent. Finance may be using simple forecasting, and teaching institution-oriented physicians may apply research approaches to clinical decisions or operations, but the application is inconsistent.

Stage 1: Beginner Competency Maturity Roadmap

Enterprise

- Begin organizational conversations about information, quality, data, and analytics.

Leadership

- Leadership generally is local to a particular specific department or area, isolated, and uncoordinated with others. Identify possible champions and leaders, analytic talent pools, and staff.

Targets

- Targets are local and may not contribute to or align with corporate strategic activities.

Analysts

- Analysts are isolated, untrained, and uncoordinated with others across the enterprise.

Stage 2: Localized Analytics

"Use reporting." Analytics and/or reporting are in silos.

- Pockets of analytical activity exist within the organization, but they are neither coordinated nor focused on strategic targets. The difference between pockets of application may be extreme. Data management is limited. Analytical skills are isolated, inconsistent, unmanaged, and uncoordinated between clinical and business efforts. Investment and effort are not entirely driven by strategic focus; rather, they are typically based on departmental needs.
- Certain operational systems may offer "analytical" or "C&BI" reporting or alerts. This is generally more likely in a research or teaching institution. Possible examples include simple financial indicator trending, salary minimum/maximum threshold management, or ICU/seasonal staffing models.

- Data are managed in isolated operational systems such as EMR, laboratory, radiology, or revenue cycle management systems or they are collected and managed manually.

Stage 2: Localized Competency Maturity Roadmap

Data

- Create data model of entire organizational data-collecting and -producing systems, including understanding of duplicate data, data definitions, terms, latency, quality, and issues.
- Latency of data used for primary and significant analytics activities is <1 month.

Enterprise

- Itemize and prioritize project management that may be coordinated on a localized basis.

Leadership

- Learn to apply analytics, focusing on "low-hanging fruit."

Targets

- Specific areas are identified for mature use of analytics, with major and narrowly focused successes.

Analysts

- Nurture and develop talent pools in specific areas; encourage core staff to participate in analytics and data management–related professional organizations. Staff is attending and applying information acquired through analytical conferences and webinars.

Stage 3: Analytically Aspiring

"See the value of analytics." Struggling to mobilize the organization and becoming more analytical.

- The HCO envisions a more analytical future, has established analytical capabilities, and has undertaken a few significant initiatives, but progress is slow, often because some critical DELTA factor has been difficult to implement.
- Data are generally "freed" but not normalized and have varying degrees of limiting latency. Some analytical coordination and standardization exists. External data sources are available. Strategic alignment is beginning to be undertaken.
- Critical data sources are beginning to be consolidated into the primary hospital information system (EMR), a data warehouse, or some variation with monthly or regular nonaggressive updates.
- Management is requesting reports in support of operational efficiencies and outlier identification that require diverse data sources, i.e., combined clinical and financial data (ICU acuity versus revenue), physician performance (inpatient versus outpa-

tient workload, referral patterns, test/pharmacy/radiology utilization against diagnosis), or emergency department patient demographic mix versus acuity.

Stage 3: Aspiring Competency Maturity Roadmap

Data

- A formal Data Governance/Quality Governance program is in place. The organization is actively discussing and working toward creating "one version of the truth." External data are integrated and used frequently and regularly.
- Latency of data used for primary and significant analytics activities is <2 weeks.
- Inbound and outbound exchange of EMR, laboratory, and radiology data is accomplished on demand with external providers.
- Patient matching is >99% between internal and external health information exchange systems.

Enterprise

- Coordinating council with project profiling (clinical and business impact) manages projects with a primarily organizational viewpoint, which includes managing expansion of services and capability.
- Specialized alerts are sent in near-real time.

Leadership

- Collaboration on DELTA efforts occurs across areas that drive data quality and coordination.
- Training regimens are in place for enablers, analysts, and users.

Targets

- Bending the cost curve.
- Analyzing and reducing 30-day readmissions.
- Defined and improving organization core measures.
- Maximizing Centers for Medicare & Medicaid Services reimbursement and incentives.
- Lowering business and clinical costs.
- Analyzing and reducing hospital-acquired infections.
- Profiling and prioritizing projects at an enterprise level that are coordinated down to the local level, including patient risk profiling such as readmission, with both clinical and business aspects addressed.

Analysts

- Job descriptions and career paths delineated.
- Enterprise-wide analytical standards formalized and documented.
- Shared resources made available for cross-pollination.

Stage 4: Analytically Capable

"Good at analytics." Highly data-oriented, have analytical tools, and make wide use of analytics. Lacks commitment to fully compete or use strategically.

- Organization has needed human and technological resources, applies analytics regularly, and realizes enterprise-wide clinical and business benefits. Strategic focus is not grounded in analytics, and analytics have not been turned to a competitive advantage.
- Analytical resources and techniques are developed, coordinated, and managed. Analytical skills are embedded across all areas, such as nursing administration, facility services, finance, social work, and radiology. Project prioritization and enterprise strategy are aligned with and supported by analytical insights and efforts.
- Historical and current data are available for clinical and business operations in a combined solution that address data governance and quality. Historical patient volume, patient census, procedure mix, ancillary service utilization, and other healthcare and operational data are regularly used for management and planning.
- Common tools, techniques, and even people are shared enterprise-wide to address needs above and beyond those offered in "commercial off-the-shelf" solutions.

Stage 4: Capable Competency Maturity Roadmap

Data

- Data exchange (internal and external discrete exchange) is pervasive for laboratory, pharmacy, and EMR on a regional, statewide, and national basis.
- Persistent health information exchange is available 24x7x365 (downtime allowed).
- Latency of data used for primary and significant analytics activities is <24 hours.

Enterprise

- Analytics standards are documented, published, refined, and maintained.
- Internal and external care coordination are consistent, timely, and seamless.
- Pervasive and effective alerts are in use.
- Proactive risk and health management is in place.

Leadership

- All leadership is engaged and using standard analytical and data resources.
- Alignment and accountability of analytical resources are demonstrated.
- Leaders are comfortable with pervasive use of analytics activities.

Targets

- Characterized and aligned with organizational strategy.
- Population health management analytics, which can include accountable care organizations, value-based purchasing, and capitated rates/services.
- Use of analytics to identity cost, revenue, patient health, clinical and business risk factor stratification, and opportunity profiling.
- Assessment of clinical and business impact on all projects using standard analytical approach, including ongoing and retrospective review(s).

Analysts

- Managed inventory of enterprise-wide analytical talent and resources is available.
- Pods of clinical/business/technical subject matter experts are used to expedite and optimize project performance.
- Analytical skills are managed and embedded across broad areas of the HCO.

Stage 5: Analytical Leader

"Analytical nirvana." Use analytics across the enterprise as a competitive differentiator and as a strategic driver.

- The HCO routinely uses analytics as a distinctive capability. It takes an enterprise-wide approach, has committed and involved leadership, and has achieved large-scale results. It portrays itself both internally and externally as an analytical competitor.
- The use of analytics is consistent, standard, and common practice for all meaningful efforts. Analytics are expected to be used to justify significant decisions and efforts. Executives regularly use advanced census, financial, acuity, and other data for trending and forecasting, sharing and promoting this information with hospital management and board leadership.
- Strategic initiatives, such as facility or service line expansion/contraction, are identified based on analytics insights. Analytics are used to identify and evaluate competitive opportunities, such as physician practice purchase, geographic information service for evaluating regional health standings, and population health risks.
- Internal and external data, such as state health department, local/federal government, census, or purchased data, are integrated into analytics activities.

Stage 5: Leader Competency Maturity Roadmap

Data

- Supports analysis for selecting and executing strategic actions.

Enterprise

- Portrayed internally and externally as an analytical organization.
- Extends analytical tools broadly and deeply across the enterprise.

Leadership

- Sees analytics as a method of anticipating and taking advantage of opportunities.
- Leverages internal and external data sets.
- Derives new and creative ways to leverage analytics and C&BI for competitive advantage.

Targets

- Analytical activities and data that are critical to success of new initiatives and activities.

Analysts

- Analytically oriented justification is expected from all levels of management.
- Strategic initiatives are assessed for analytical requirements and data needs and used to track performance and measure success.

REFERENCES

1. Davenport TH, Harris JG. *Competing on Analytics: The New Science of Winning.* Boston, MA: Harvard Business School Publishing Corporation; 2007.

2. Davenport TH, Harris JG, Morison R. *Analytics at Work: Smarter Decisions, Better Results.* Boston, MA: Harvard Business School Publishing Corporation; 2010.

3. Analytics. *Wikipedia.* 2013. http://en.wikipedia.org/wiki/Analytics. Accessed December 2013.

4. *Electronic Medical Record Adoption Model (EMRAM)^{SM}.* Chicago, IL: HIMSS Analytics; 2013. http://www.himssanalytics.org/emram/emram.aspx. Accessed December 2013.

5. *Ambulatory EMR Adoption Model^{SM}.* Chicago, IL: HIMSS Analytics; 2013. http://www.himssanalytics.org/emram/AEMRAM.aspx. Accessed December 2013.

6. *About IIA: The Authority on Analytics Maturity and Best Practices.* Portland, OR: International Institute for Analytics. http://iianalytics.com/about-iia/. Accessed December 2013.

CHAPTER 9

Conclusions

Raymond A. Gensinger, Jr.

HEALTHCARE ANALYTICS WRAP-UP

In the time that it has taken you to read through this book, another dozen companies likely have entered into the healthcare analytics marketplace and five times that number of new articles have been published. For just that reason, we have tried to walk you through a fundamental approach to analytics in the healthcare space. The DELTA Analytics Maturity Model presented in Chapter 8 offers one approach to measuring your level of analytic maturity and offers assistance with achieving that maturation. The companies and articles cited throughout the book likely offer additional approaches with similar intents.

Chapters 1 through 3 introduced analytics and business intelligence history and argued for the use of analytics in today's healthcare marketplace. To understand the healthcare business fully, determine efficient and effective care of patients, and perhaps even address that group of "pre-patients" falling into accountable care organizations, we need to understand and predict the next steps. These include managing the sickest patients more effectively, determining which current patients will become really sick patients next year, and ascertaining those factors that will turn patients down a path of disease rather than one of wellness and longevity. To this end, we explored several existing meaningful use cases in these chapters to apply analytics to our changing healthcare paradigm.

In Chapter 4, we dove into some of the analytics challenges that are clearly evident in the near term, such as practical big data challenges that will arise as we consider the addition of genotypic data to accompany existing phenotypic data. That consideration introduces further challenges in data storage and processing strategies that must be addressed. We additionally introduced the opportunities and challenges of the "spoken word" and how we might unlock the context of free clinical text as a part of the analytic framework. Finally, we shared some of the many different approaches by which the output of such analyses will need to be delivered to specialty providers and consumers.

Chapter 5 illustrated the power of analytics at work through the advanced analytic discipline of data mining. We shared the results of several research studies that used real clinical data from electronic health records to demonstrate the power of the data we hold when it is shared with experts in data mining. Although such projects are not intended for the casual analytics operation, they demonstrate the potential for combining data from numerous organizations to yield further power to analyses.

Chapters 6 and 7 addressed the more practical side of analytics. Armed with a rejuvenated knowledge and understanding of the capabilities of a mature analytics and business intelligence program, we related the practical elements and foundations necessary for success. Chapter 6 examined the leadership roles and organizational structures that have been successful in other industries. We discussed the pros and cons of various options and began to discuss the types of competencies needed to ensure success. Leaders may not have previously considered some of these responsibilities or been aware of roles that have not previously existed in the healthcare industry.

Chapter 7 detailed the management of data. Data governance and data management disciplines are likely to be at varying levels of maturity, based on the overall maturity of the organization. Regardless of any organization's current starting point, the chapter offered the specific details of policy, procedure, and governance designed to help them succeed.

Finally, Chapter 8 reviewed a specific service opportunity offered by HIMSS Analytics. That offering is built upon the DELTA model that has been referenced repeatedly throughout this book. HIMSS Analytics, in partnership with the International Institute of Analytics, have leveraged the DELTA model in a way for you to assess your organizational maturity and readiness to excel.

ONE LAST WORD

In the time it has taken me to write this conclusion, yet another article on analytics has hit the presses. Davenport reports in *Harvard Business Review* on the next evolution of analytics in industry.[1] Think not just about gathering data that are passively accumulating in your surroundings, but consider the opportunity to put additional "sensors" into your environment and begin to capture additional data with the purposes of further understanding and adding efficiencies to your business and its related workflows.

For healthcare, this could be considered as an alternative to time/motion studies that are typically manually recorded. Consider the opportunity to apply real-time monitoring to staff and patients for better understanding of choke points or inefficiencies in workflow as well as how staff interacts with patient call lights, family and visitor interactions, and the overall processes of patient care. This next generation of analytics suggests the possibility of enhancing the power of data by continuing to add new dimensions for yet newer insights.

Data, analytics, and the insights and predictions that they illuminate are here to stay. The other authors and I hope that we have been able to provide you with additional insights and a sufficient starter set of suggestions to help you begin to move your organization to its next evolution of healthcare analytics.

REFERENCE

1.   Davenport TH. Analytics 3.0. *Harvard Business Review*. December 2013. http://hbr.org/2013/12/
      analytics-30/ar/1. Accessed December 2013.

Secondary Use of Data: Learning Modules For Healthcare Providers: A Missing Piece

Nathaniel A. Wells

Analytics allow for real-time assessment and adjustment to issues, problems, and services across multiple industries. Professional sports teams use analytics for real-time adjustments in game strategy. Businesses use analytics to provide just-in-time value-added services. Industries now are focusing on marketing improved services to their customers. This approach is exemplified by the expression, "The new boss is the customer" and emphasized via television commercials claiming, "We can build a better planet" (IBM) and "Things can always be better!" (Honda). Healthcare providers must follow this trend by concentrating on their customers, who are their patients. They can accomplish this goal by following the example of business in using data to make sound decisions.

EDUCATING HEALTHCARE PROVIDERS

The opportunity offered by secondary use of data to "see around corners" can be hindered by a lack of understanding about how to use data. To address this gap in knowledge, we created learning modules that include expected outcomes. This curriculum can be used to assess the knowledge base of healthcare providers and subsequently educate them about strategies of data usage and analysis. The information ranges from the underlying philosophy and available tools to thinking of the data within a cost-benefit context and providing justifications for why providers should become familiar with data analysis and use it in population healthcare strategies.

One anticipated challenge is the need for providers to think about and manage data at both a population level and an individual patient level. Further, providers may be challenged by limited experience in several areas: (1) incorporation of constraints, expert knowledge, and/or background knowledge in data mining, pattern evaluation, and knowledge integration; (2) knowledge discovery through inquiry and interaction with data scientists who do not necessarily have clinical backgrounds; and

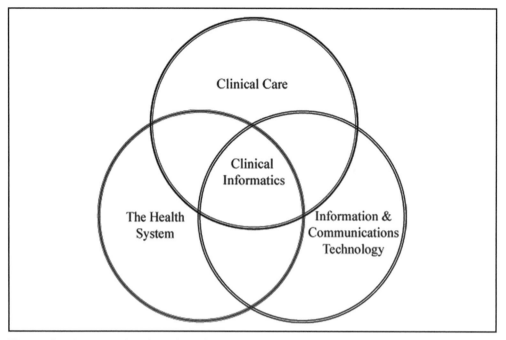

Figure A-1: Intersecting domains of clinical informatics.

(3) a thorough understanding of the value of business intelligence and its application in healthcare.

Helping providers deliver proactive, effective, and appropriate care should be best practice for healthcare organizations. Providers should understand basic philosophies behind electronic health record (EHR) data entry, storage, and analysis. In other words, they must understand where informatics live within their professions (Figure A-1).[1]

The following sample curriculum can be incorporated into an existing organizational learning curriculum. The goal is to bring staff to a common understanding of the basics of informatics related to data and analytics in healthcare. The curriculum can serve as a starting point for an organization beginning an analytics journey.

CURRICULUM

Module 1 - Health informatics: big data, big possibilities.

Goal: Provide an introductory overview on the use, credibility, quality, and potential of big data through examination of:

- Data analytics—Power and value of big data in population health.
- Data utilization—The importance of understanding, knowledge discovery, data mining, and business intelligence.
- Informatics and implications of data.
- Population health data—Potential use for high-value care.

Objectives

Upon completion, the student will be able to:

1. Define big data.
2. Draw literature-supported conclusions on the effectiveness of data use in healthcare.
3. Define data-driven decision-making (DDDM) implementation value, including facilitations and hindrances.
4. List five research-supported methods of leveraging big data.
5. State future competitive advantages or disadvantages with the use of big data.

Student Activities

- Complete short pretest questionnaire.
- Read prescribed literature.
- Complete post-test questionnaire.
- Write a brief reflection statement on what student has learned.

Module 2 – Identification and recognition of patterns—the data speak.

Goal: Promote pattern evaluation and knowledge integration of providers.

- Questions to ask, such as "Do I have the right results?"
- Understanding of agreed-upon best practices balanced with cost.
- Role of clinical decision support, technology acceptance model (TAM)
- Linkage blindness for trend identification and case compatibility across system.

Module 3 – A new model for coding. How the provider can help assure the codes are accurate.

Goal: Promote understanding of interrelated information uses for financial success in reimbursements.

- Coding
- International Statistical Classification of Diseases, 10th revision (ICD-10) quality assurance

Module 4 – Strategies surrounding the appropriate handling of data that you will need to use again.

Goal: Establish a mindset for good habits during medical records information entry.

- Garbage in, garbage out
- Normalization
- Responsibility for discrete data capture (natural language processing)
- Transaction processing
- Why quality?
- How clinicians can help clean and shape output at the beginning

Module 5 – Data and big data database terminologies, storage solutions, maintenance, and processing approaches.
Goal: Gain an understanding of the data mining lifecycle.
- Extraction, transformation & load
- Data warehouse
- Harmonization
- Big data, data mining

Module 6 – Statistical programs and applications used in business intelligence.
Goal: Learn how information is processed to promote trust in analytic information.
- Statistical packages – SAS, R, Excel, SPSS, STATA, etc.

Module 7 – Visualizing information with a quick glance and without seeing the data.
Goal: Promote knowledge discovery through inquiry and interaction with data scientists and the outputs they produce.
- Descriptive analytics
- Charts/dashboards/graphs
- Modeling
- Scorecards

Module 8 – Statistics and other metrics meaningful for population analyses.
Goal: Gain an understanding of statistical and research quality assurance.
- Sensitivity, specificity, positive predictive value, negative predictive value, gold standard

Module 9 – Using data and quality measures to "see around corners."
Goal: Learn about the approach and basic philosophies behind data analysis and how they can be used in healthcare.
- Introduction to predictive and prescriptive analytics
- Insight foresight via plan-do-study-act (PDSA)
- Summary and traits
- Analysis and considerations

Module 10 – How data analytics can support the business of caring for patients.
Goal: Gain an understanding of the value of business intelligence and its application in healthcare.
- Secondary use
- Trust of analysts
- Questions to ask of data

CONTINUED LEARNING

The suggested structure of these learning modules is consistent with many of the concepts introduced in this book. They have been designed as meaningful 1-hour lessons that can be locally constructed to best meet organizational objectives while introducing the suggested concepts. As their analytics maturity grows, organizations may be interested in placing more focus on analytical understanding of the TAM,[2] quality,[3] and DDDM.[3]

Two other topics may merit more detailed information: translational bioinformatics and knowledge discovery and data mining. Translational bioinformatics involves "the development of storage, analytic, and interpretive methods to optimize the transformation of increasingly voluminous biomedical data, and genomic data into proactive, predictive, preventive, and participatory health."[4] Knowledge discovery and data mining "focuses on the process of extracting meaningful patterns from biomedical data (knowledge discovery), using automated computational and statistical tools and techniques on large datasets (data mining). Its underlying goal is to help humans make high-level sense of large volumes of low-level data and share that knowledge with colleagues in related fields."[5] The American Medical Informatics Association has two working groups that address these topics (http://www.amia.org/working-groups).

REFERENCES

1. Gardner RM, Overhage JM, Steen EB, et al; AMIA Board of Directors. Core content for the subspecialty of clinical informatics. *J Am Med Inform Assoc*. 2009;16:153-157. doi: 10.1197/jamia.M3045.

2. McAfee A, Brynjolfsson E. Big data: the management revolution. *Harv Bus Rev*. 2012;90:60-66, 68, 128.

3. Orwin RG, Edwards JM, Buchanan RM, Flewelling RL, Landy AL. Data-driven decision making in the prevention of substance-related harm: results from the Strategic Prevention Framework State Incentive Grant Program. *Contemporary Drug Problems*. 2012;39:34. https://www.federallegalpublications.com/contemporary-drug-problems/201206/cdp-2012-39-1-04-orwin-data-driven-decision-making-prevention-of-s. Accessed December 2013.

4. American Medical Informatics Association. Informatics Areas: Translational Bioinformatics website. http://www.amia.org/applications-informatics/translational-bioinformatics. Accessed December 2013.

5. American Medical Informatics Association. Working Group: Knowledge Discovery and Data Mining website. http://www.amia.org/programs/working-groups/knowledge-discovery-and-data-mining. Accessed December 2013.

SUGGESTED READINGS

American Hospital Association. *Health Care Reform Implementation Timeline*. 2010. http://www.aha.org/content/00-10/10may-reformtimeline.pdf. Accessed December 2012.

AMIA Joint Summits on Translational Science. 2012 Summit on Translational Bioinformatics. San Francisco, CA: AMIA; 2012. http://www.amia.org/sites/amia.org/files/TBI-Onsite-Program-2012-FINAL.pdf. Accessed December 2013.

Barie PS. Does a well-done analysis of poor-quality data constitute evidence of benefit? *Ann Surg*. 2012;255:1030-1031. doi: 10.1097/SLA.0b013e3182574dd3.

How does your doctor compare? *Consumer Reports/MNCM Health Insert.* 2012:1-32. http://mnhealthscores.org/news/assets/CR-MNCM insert FINAL.pdf. Accessed December 2013.

Improving Health Outcomes. Chicago, IL: American Medical Association; 2012. http://www.ama-assn.org/resources/doc/about-ama/improving-health-outcomes.pdf. Accessed December 2013.

Marsolo K. Informatics and operations—let's get integrated. *J Am Med Inform Assoc.* 2013;20:122-124. doi: 10.1136/amiajnl-2012-001194.

McGuire T, Manyika J, Chui M. Why big data is the new competitive advantage. *Ivey Business Journal.* 2012;76(4):1-4. http://iveybusinessjournal.com/topics/strategy/why-big-data-is-the-new-competitive-advantage#.UsLy_42A3Z4. Accessed December 2013.

Ohno-Machado L. To share or not to share: that is not the question. *Sci Transl Med.* 2012;4(165):165cm15. doi: 10.1126/scitranslmed.3004454.

Pentland A. Big data's biggest obstacles. *HBR Blog Network.* [Internet]. 2012. http://blogs.hbr.org/cs/2012/10/big_datas_biggest_obstacles.html. Accessed December 2013.

Schadt EE, Linderman MD, Sorenson J, Lee L, Nolan GP. Computational solutions to large-scale data management and analysis. *Nat Rev Genet.* 201011:647-657. doi: 10.1038/nrg2857.

10x10 with University of Minnesota School of Nursing: *Interprofessional Health Informatics Course.*: http://www.amia.org/education/10x10-courses/10x10-umn/course-description. Accessed December 2013.

Glossary

Accountable care organizations (ACO) An umbrella term for a major switch in contracting between providers and public or private payers. In an ACO model, a group of providers, operating as a legal entity, contracts to assume some portion of the risk for cost and quality for a panel of beneficiaries through a variety of value-based payment models over a specified period of time. ACOs include primary care services. The U.S. CMS Distributed Shared Savings Program, which began operation in 2012, is one version of this model.
http://www.gartner.com/it-glossary

Ad hoc reporting Reports generated for a one-time need.
http://data-informed.com/glossary-of-big-data-terms/

Algorithm (general) A mathematical formula placed in software that performs an analysis on a set of data.
http://data-informed.com/glossary-of-big-data-terms/
http://xlinux.nist.gov/dads//HTML/segment.html
http://pic.dhe.ibm.com/infocenter/spssstat/v20r0m0/index.jsp?topic=%2Fcom.ibm.spss. statistics.help%2Falg_regression.htm

Association algorithms Algorithms that find correlations between different attributes in a dataset. The most common application of this kind of algorithm is for creating association rules, which can be used in a market basket analysis.

BI analytics environment Enables enterprises to build BI applications by providing capabilities in three categories: analysis, such as online analytical processing (OLAP); information delivery, such as reports and dashboards; and platform integration, such as BI metadata management and a development environment.
http://www.gartner.com/it-glossary

Big data High-volume, high-velocity and high-variety information assets that demand cost-effective, innovative forms of information processing for enhanced insight and decision making.
http://www.vertica.com/resources/data-analytics-glossary/
http://data-informed.com/glossary-of-big-data-terms/

Bolt-on environments   Used to describe products and systems that can be quickly but securely attached to an existing environments.

Bundled payment schemes (bundling)   Defined as the practice of packaging multiple features and products together for a single price.
http://www.gartner.com/it-glossary

Business intelligence (BI)   The general term used for the identification, extraction, and analysis of data. An umbrella term that includes the applications, infrastructure and tools, and best practices that enable access to and analysis of information to improve and optimize decisions and performance.
http://www.vertica.com/resources/data-analytics-glossary/
http://data-informed.com/glossary-of-big-data-terms/

Central registry   Files of one or more organizational units stored in one physical location to improve their management and control.

Classification algorithms   Algorithms that predict one or more discrete variables, based on the other attributes in the dataset.

Clinical decision support (CDS)   Typically used when referring to a type of system that assists healthcare providers in making medical decisions. These types of systems typically require input of patient-specific clinical variables and as a result provide patient-specific recommendations.
http://www.hl7.org/documentcenter/public_temp_A3CC0E7C-1C23-BA17-0C4857E00747DC4F/calendarofevents/FirstTime/Glossary%20of%20terms.pdf

Clinical messaging system   Any electronic system that allows the transfer of clinical data such as laboratory tests, radiology results, transcriptions, prescriptions, and clinical orders quickly from provider to provider.
http://www.himss.org/files/HIMSSorg/content/files/2009HIEGUIDEGlossary.pdf

Cluster algorithms   CLUSTER produces hierarchical clusters of items based on distance measures of dissimilarity or similarity.

Control chart   A chart with upper and lower control limits on which values of some statistical measure for a series of samples or subgroups are plotted. The chart frequently shows a central line to help detect a trend of plotted values toward either control limit.

Correlation   A measure of the relationship between two data sets of variables.
http://www.cochrane.org/glossary
http://www.mc.vanderbilt.edu/root/vumc.php?site=qicourse&doc=11718

Dashboard   A data visualization tool that displays the current status of metrics and key performance indicators (KPIs) for an enterprise. They consolidate and arrange numbers, metrics and sometimes performance scorecards on a single screen.
http://data-informed.com/glossary-of-big-data-terms/
http://www.gartner.com/it-glossary

Data fragmentation When related data in is broken up into many parts that are not stored close together. Often results in missed connections and wasted storage space.
http://itlaw.wikia.com/wiki/Data_fragmentation

Data governance The exercise of decision-making and authority for data-related matters. The organizational bodies, rules, decision rights, and accountabilities of people and information systems as they perform information-related processes. Data governance determines how an organization makes decisions—how we "decide how to decide."
http://data-informed.com/glossary-of-big-data-terms/

Data integrator Software enabling organizations to extract, transform, and load data from inside and outside its firewall.
http://www.gartner.com/it-glossary

Data marts A database that is similar in structure to a data warehouse, but is typically smaller and is focused on a more limited subject area. Multiple, integrated data marts are sometimes referred to as an integrated data warehouse. Data marts may be used in place of a larger data warehouse or in conjunction with it. They are typically less expensive to develop and faster to deploy and are therefore becoming more popular with smaller organizations.
http://data-informed.com/glossary-of-big-data-terms/

Data matrix (mathematics) (plural: matrices) A rectangular array of numbers, symbols, or expressions, arranged in rows and column.

Data mining The process of researching data marts and data warehouses to detect specific patterns in the data sets. Data mining may be performed on databases and multi-dimensional data cubes with ad hoc query tools and OLAP software. The queries and reports are typically designed to answer specific questions to uncover trends or hidden relationships in the data.
http://data-informed.com/glossary-of-big-data-terms/

Data modeling The discipline, process, and organizational group that conducts analysis of data objects used in a business or other context, identifies the relationships among these data objects, and creates models that depict those relationships.
http://data-informed.com/glossary-of-big-data-terms/
http://www.vertaasis.com/glossary.php

Data parser The process of analyzing a string of symbols, either in natural language or in computer languages, according to the rules of a formal grammar.

Data stewardship Encompasses the responsibilities and accountabilities associated with managing, collecting, viewing, storing, sharing, disclosing, or otherwise making use of personal health information. Principles of data stewardship apply to all the personnel, systems and processes engaging in health information storage and exchange within and across organizations.

Data visualization   The creation and study of the visual representation of data, meaning "information that has been abstracted in some schematic form, including attributes or variables for the units of information."

Data warehouse   An integrated, non-volatile database of historical information that is designed around specific content areas and is used to answer questions regarding an organization's operations and environment.
http://www.gartner.com/it-glossary/data-warehouse

Decision support   A set of queries, reports, rule-based analyses, tables and charts that are designed to aid management with their decision-making responsibilities. These functions are typically "wrapped around" a data mart or data warehouse. The DSS tends to employ more detailed level data than an EIS.

Descriptive analytics (optimization and simulation)   Considers data and analyzes past events for insight as to how to approach the future.
http://www.rosebt.com/1/post/2012/08/predictive-descriptive-prescriptive-analytics.html

Dimension   A variable, perspective or general category of information that is used to organize and analyze information in a multidimensional data cube.
http://pic.dhe.ibm.com/infocenter/spssstat/v20r0m0/index.jsp?topic=%2Fcom.ibm.spss.statistics.help%2Falg_regression.htm

Drilldown   The ability of a data-mining tool to move down into increasing levels of detail in a data mart, data warehouse or multidimensional data cube.

Electronic medical record (EMR)   A digital version of the paper charts in the clinician's office. Contains the medical and treatment history of the patients in one practice. (ONCHIT)
http://www.himss.org/News/NewsDetail.aspx?ItemNumber=6776
http://www.himss.org/files/HIMSSorg/content/files/2009HIEGUIDEGlossary.pdf

Enterprise data warehouses (EDW)   An EDW aggregates and organizes data from throughout the entire organization.
http://www.vertica.com/resources/data-analytics-glossary/

Enterprise master patient indices (EMPIs)   A database that is used across a healthcare organization to maintain consistent, accurate and current demographic and essential medical data on the patients seen and managed within its various departments.
http://en.wikipedia.org/wiki/Enterprise_master_patient_index

Extract-transform-load (ETL)   To extract data from a data source like an operational system or data warehouse, modify the data and then load it into a data mart, data warehouse or multidimensional data cube.

Forecasts   A prediction or estimate of future events.

Heterogeneous data elements   Data elements of differing types that are logically related.
http://wiki.answers.com/Q/What_is_heterogeneous_data#slide3
http://courses.cs.vt.edu/~cs1044/fall02/mcpherson/notes/c10.structures.pdf

Hierarchy   The organization of data, e.g., a dimension, into an outline or logical tree structure. The strata of a hierarchy are referred to as levels. The individual elements within a level are referred to as categories. The next lower level in a hierarchy is the child; the next higher level containing the children is their parent.

HL7   Health Level Seven (HL7) is an application protocol for electronic data exchange in health care environments. The HL7 protocol is a collection of standard formats which specify the implementation of interfaces between computer applications from different vendors. This communication protocol allows healthcare institutions to exchange key sets of data among different application systems. Flexibility is built into the protocol to allow compatibility for specialized data sets that have facility-specific needs.
http://www.hl7.org/documentcenter/public_temp_A3CC0E7C-1C23-BA17-0C4857E00747DC4F/calendarofevents/FirstTime/Glossary%20of%20terms.pdf

ICD-10   ICD-10 codes must be used on all HIPAA transactions, including outpatient claims with dates of service, and inpatient claims with dates of discharge on and after October 1, 2014.
http://www.cms.gov
http://himss.files.cms-plus.com/HIMSSorg/Content/files/Code%20147_Quality%20101%20-%20Definitions-Glossary%20of%20Terms_HIMSS.pdf

ICD-9   A coding system for medical diagnoses, symptoms, and nonspecific complaints. It is frequently used on insurance claim forms to identify the reasons for providing medical services.
http://www.cms.gov

Internet of Everything (IoE)   The intelligent connection of people, processes, data and things, making network connections more relevant and valuable than ever before, resulting in new capabilities, better business decisions, the creation of unprecedented economic value, richer experiences and improved quality of life.
http://blogs.cisco.com/ioe/how-the-internet-of-everything-will-change-the-world-for-the-better-infographic/

Internet of Objects   See Internet of Things (IoT).

Internet of Things (IoT)   The network of physical objects that contains embedded technology to communicate and sense or interact with their internal states or the external environment.
http://www.cisco.com/web/tomorrow-starts-here/ioe/index.html?POSITION=SEM&COUNTRY_SITE=us&CAMPAIGN=tomorrowstartshere&CREATIVE=SL_Brand&REFERRING_SITE=Google&KEYWORD=SL+Internet+of+Everything_s|mkwid_sK9YuYOia|dc_SITELINK_0v0xx7y7d0

Joint Commission, The   A U.S. healthcare accreditation body; formerly known as Joint Commission on the Accreditation of Hospitals and Healthcare Organizations.

Laboratory Information Management Systems (LIMS)   A solution to manage sample scientific test data and processes, from sample login to the reporting of results.

Logical data model   Any data model where a particular method of organization is used to organize data. Examples are the relational, hierarchical, network and object data models.
http://www.dr-mikes-maths.com/database-glossary.html

Multidimensional databases   A database management system that stores and manages data in dimensional arrays, indexed by dimensions and measured over time.

Normalization   The process of eliminating duplicate information in a database by creating a separate table that stores the redundant information. For example, it would be highly inefficient to re-enter the address of an insurance company with every claim. Instead, the database uses a key field to link the claims table to the address table. Operational or transaction processing systems are typically "normalized." On the other hand, some data warehouses find it advantageous to de-normalize the data allowing for some degree of redundancy.
http://www.dr-mikes-maths.com/database-glossary.html
http://www.vertaasis.com/glossary.php

Normalization algorithm   An algorithm for taking an unnormalized relation and putting it into a higher normal form.
http://www.dr-mikes-maths.com/database-glossary.html

Ontology   A rigorous and exhaustive organization of some knowledge domain that is usually hierarchical and contains all the relevant entities and their relationships.
http://www.merriam-webster.com/dictionary/ontology
http://www.expertglossary.com/knowledge-management/definitions/O

Phenotyping algorithms   Algorithm applied to an organism's observable characteristics or traits.

Pivot tables   A data summarization tool found in data visualization programs such as spreadsheets or business intelligence software.

Population health   The health outcomes of a group of individuals, including the distribution of such outcomes within the group.

Predictive analytics (*forecasting*)   Describes any approach to data mining with four attributes: an emphasis on prediction (rather than description, classification or clustering); rapid analysis measured in hours or days (rather than the stereotypical months of traditional data mining); an emphasis on the business relevance of the resulting insights (no ivory tower analyses); and (increasingly) an emphasis on ease of use, thus making the tools accessible to business users. Predictive analytics leverages data mining to identify trends and variables that can be used to predict future events, behaviors and outcomes.
http://www.rosebt.com/1/post/2012/08/predictive-descriptive-prescriptive-analytics.html

Predictive model   A commonly used statistical technique to predict future behavior. Predictive modeling solutions are a form of data-mining technology that work by analyzing historical and current data and generating a model to help predict future outcomes. In predictive modeling, data are collected, a statistical model is formulated, predictions are made, and the model is validated (or revised) as additional data become available. For example, risk models can be created to combine member information in complex ways with demographic and lifestyle information from external sources to improve underwriting accuracy. Predictive models analyze past performance to assess how likely a customer is to exhibit a specific behavior in the future. This category also encompasses models that seek out subtle data patterns to answer questions about customer performance, such as fraud detection models. Predictive models often perform calculations during live transactions—for example, to evaluate the risk or opportunity of a given customer or transaction to guide a decision. If health insurers could accurately predict secular trends (for example, utilization), premiums would be set appropriately, profit targets would be met with more consistency, and health insurers would be more competitive in the marketplace.

http://www.rosebt.com/1/post/2012/08/predictive-descriptive-prescriptive-analytics.html

Prescriptive analytics *(business intelligence and data mining)* Synthesizes big data, mathematical sciences, business rules, and machine learning to make predictions and then suggests decision options to take advantage of the predictions.

http://www.rosebt.com/1/post/2012/08/predictive-descriptive-prescriptive-analytics.html

Readmission reduction Reduction of an admission to a subsection(d) hospital within 30 days of a discharge from the same or another subsection(d) hospital. (CMS)

Readmission risk model A model to measure a patient's risk for an inpatient readmission within a predetermined time frame of a primary inpatient event.

http://www.empireblue.com/provider/noapplication/f1/s0/t0/pw_e192617.pdf?refer=ehpprovider

Regression algorithm Predicts one or more continuous variables, such as profit or loss, based on other attributes in the dataset. This procedure performs multiple linear regression with five methods for entry and removal of variables. It also provides extensive analysis of residual and influential cases. Caseweight (CASEWEIGHT) and regression weight (REGWGT) can be specified in the model fitting.

http://pic.dhe.ibm.com/infocenter/spssstat/v20r0m0/index.jsp?topic=%2Fcom.ibm.spss.statistics.help%2Falg_regression.htm

Scorecard An evaluation device, usually in the form of a questionnaire, that specifies the criteria customers will use to rate your business performance in satisfying customer requirements.

http://www.mc.vanderbilt.edu/root/vumc.php?site=qicourse&doc=11718

Segmentation algorithm Divides data into groups, or clusters, of items that have similar properties.

http://xlinux.nist.gov/dads//HTML/segment.html

Simulation The use of a mathematical or computer representation of a physical system for the purpose of studying constraint effects.

Structured Data Data that are identifiable because they are organized in a structure.

Structured query language (SQL)   A standard language, the structured query language, incorporating DDL and DML features, used to manipulate databases. Available in most commercial RDBMSs.
http://www.vertica.com/resources/data-analytics-glossary/
http://www.dr-mikes-maths.com/database-glossary.html

Table de-normalization   The process of attempting to optimize the read performance of a database by adding redundant data or by grouping data.

Transactional information systems   See electronic medical record (EMR).
http://www.gartner.com/it-glossary

Unstructured data   Any data that has no identifiable structure.
http://www.vertica.com/resources/data-analytics-glossary/

Table of Acronyms

ACA	Affordable Care Act
ACO	accountable care organization
BI	business intelligence
BICC	business intelligence competency center
C&BI	clinical and business intelligence
CDS	clinical decision support
CMS	Centers for Medicare & Medicaid Services
CPT	current procedural terminology
DDDM	data-derived decision-making
DRG	diagnosis-related group
EDW	enterprise data warehouses
EHR	electronic health record
EMPI	enterprise master patient index
EMR	electronic medical record
EMRAM	EMR adoption model
ETL	extraction, transformation, & load
FTE	full-time equivalency
FTP	file transfer protocol
GPOS	group purchasing organizations
HCO	healthcare organization
HHS	United States Department of Health and Human Services
HIM	health information management
HIMSS	Healthcare Information and Management Systems Society
HIPAA	Health Insurance Portability and Accountability Act

HITECH	health information technology for economic and clinical health
HITSP	Health Information Technology Standards Panel
HMO	health maintenance organization
ICD-10	International Statistical Classification of Diseases, 10th revision
ICD-9	International Statistical Classification of Diseases, 9th revision
ICU	intensive care unit
IIA	International Institute for Analytics
IT	information technology
KPI	key performance indicator
LDW	logical data warehouse
MDM	master data management
NLP	natural language processing
OPPE	Ongoing Professional Practice Evaluation
PDSA	plan-do-study-act
PRO	patient-reported outcome
QA	quality assurance
ROI	return on investment
SME	subject matter expert
SQL	Structured query language
TAM	technology acceptance model
T2DM	type 2 diabetes mellitus

Index

f = figure
t = table

A

accountable care organization (ACO), 6–7, 14, 16, 19, 20, 68*t*, 96, 97
Affordable Care Act (ACA), 19, 71, 87
analytics infrastructure, 21, 24–27, 41, 65*t*
analytics platforms, 43
authorization of data use, 72

B

benchmarking, 7, 8–9, 83, 86, 88
BICC. See business intelligence competency center (BICC).
big data, defined, 4–6
big data computing, 36, 37*t*, 44, 85, 100–102
big data consumers, 62
bioinformatics, 37–40, 103
business intelligence (BI), 13, 14, 15–20, 27, 59, 60, 83, 102, 103
    defined, 15
    descriptive, 10, 15, 16, 20, 22, 23*f*, 64, 102
    predictive, 10, 15, 17–18, 19, 20, 22, 23, 30, 32, 64, 66, 68*t*, 85, 102, 103
    prescriptive, 10, 15, 18–19, 20, 22, 23, 30, 32, 64, 66, 68*t*, 85, 102, 103
business intelligence and analytics, 75
business intelligence competency center (BICC), 59–70
    defined, 60
    functions, 61–62
    key roles and expertise, 63–66
    leadership, 66–69
    project sponsorship, 67–69
    staffing, 62–63, 67*f*
    strategic alignment, 67, 68*t*

C

care managers, 7, 19
case management, 9–10, 20
case studies, 30–33, 51–56
C&BI. See clinical & business intelligence (C&BI).

T

V

W